WHEN CUBA CONQUERED KENTUCKY

WHEN CUBA CONQUERED KENTUCKY

MARIANNE WALKER

Rutledge Hill Press®
Nashville, Tennessee

All rights reserved. Written permission must be secured from the publisher to use or reproduce any part of this book, except for brief quotations in critical reviews and articles.

Published in Nashville, Tennessee, by Rutledge Hill Press®, 211 Seventh Avenue North, Nashville, Tennessee 37219.

Distributed in Canada by H. B. Fenn & Company, Ltd., 34 Nixon Road, Bolton, Ontario L7E 1W2.

Distributed in Australia by The Five Mile Press Pty., Ltd., 22 Summit Road, Noble Park, Victoria 3174.

Distributed in New Zealand by Tandem Press, 2 Rugby Road, Birkenhead, Auckland 10.

Distributed in the United Kingdom by Verulam Publishing, Ltd., 152a Park Street Lane, Park Street, St. Albans, Hertfordshire AL2 2AU.

Typography by E. T. Lowe Publishing Company.

Team photo on page xv from Cuba school yearbook, *The Echo '52*.

Library of Congress Cataloging-in-Publication Data is available.

ISBN:1-55853-745-7

Printed in the United States of America

1 2 3 4 5 6 7 8 9—02 01 00 99

To my grandsons:
William Walker Bailey, eleven years old,
who loves sports and books,
and
Thomas Walker Jones, five months old,
who, I hope, will love sports and books

CONTENTS

PREFACE

One fall afternoon in 1988, my friend Pam Thomas and I were talking about an article that I had written for the *Louisville Courier-Journal Sunday Magazine*. She surprised me when she said that my next article ought to be about basketball. Although we had had many conversations, sports had never been the topic of any of them. Looking askance at her, I replied, "Basketball? Why in the world would I want to write about that? I don't do sports!" Pam and I are English teachers who have heard, preached, and practiced that axiom "Write about what you know." Little did I realize then that my being outside the athletic arena was an advantage to me as a writer, for I have been able to bring to this sports story a different and needed perspective.

At the time Pam made her suggestion, she was married to Howard Crittenden, and she asked if I knew that Howard had been an outstanding basketball player in both high school and college. She explained that the small country school he had attended was in a tiny place called Cuba in the far western part of Kentucky, in a region known as the Jackson Purchase; that his basketball team went to the state tournament one year and lost, then came back the next year and won. Representing one of the smallest rural schools in the state, Howard and his fellow Cuba Cubs beat one of the largest schools in the state in 1952 to win the state title. Not only that, she added, but basketball fans loved them because of the way they played basketball—they imitated the Harlem Globetrotters. "I think if you talked to Howard and some of the others from that team and saw where they grew up and where they played basketball," she said, "I'll bet you would find some good material to write about."

I was doubtful. At the time I was deeply immersed in research for a biography I was writing of Margaret Mitchell, author of *Gone With the Wind*. The idea of writing a piece about a basketball team did not interest me, but as a courtesy to my friend, I agreed to look into the subject. And when I did, I found that Pam was right—there was great material for a story here.

The result of my first research efforts was a feature article entitled "When Cuba Conquered Kentucky," which appeared in the February 26, 1989, edition of the *Louisville Courier-Journal Sunday Magazine*. The article, which drew plenty of nice reactions from readers, was a straight journalistic account of the *facts* of the Cuba Cubs' success. It told only the who, what, when, where, why, and how of the story. I knew then that at some later point I would need to get back to the Cubs to let them finish telling me their whole story so I could flesh it out with feelings and perspective. *I wanted to hear their interpretation of the facts. I wanted to listen to their voices telling their story.* It is a compelling story about the triumphant human spirit; about the human capacity to dream, hope, work, and succeed despite great disadvantages; and about the manner in which the land shapes the lives and personalities of the people who live on it. Cuba's story is worth preserving as much more than a tale about winning basketball games.

After my Margaret Mitchell biography was published in late 1993, I spent much of the next two years traveling around making presentations on Mitchell and *Gone With the Wind*, in addition to my teaching job. By 1997, when things began to settle down, I decided to use my spare time to again focus on the Cuba Cubs. I am grateful to Dr. Patrick Lake, president of Henderson (Kentucky) Community College, where I teach, for granting me a sabbatical leave for one semester that year so I could start my research. Finding material, however, was not as easy as I had naively thought it would be. I couldn't just turn to books for the kind of history I needed, nor were there available family letters and papers as there had been for the Mitchell project.

Tracking down people who had lived in Graves County in the thirties, forties, and fifties—people I needed to talk to—was not easy. Then, after finding many of them, getting them to talk was another problem. I had to earn their confidence before they answered any questions. More often than not, their answers just led to more questions and more searches. Information came in bits and pieces, often wrapped up in random, tangled narratives. Each memory tapped contained layers and layers that had to be individually peeled back. There were times this project seemed impossible. Yet I couldn't let go of it, especially after I learned of the disadvantages these people had endured. A source of my persistence was some of the Cuba players themselves, who had told me that their coach, Jack Story, had always taught them to never quit. "Don't give up!" Coach Story told his Cubs. "The only time you lose is when you quit!" Hearing that, I knew I couldn't quit. So I persisted in drawing out this story over time.

Many people were generous in their giving of time and resources so that I could write this book. Memories were shared, as were treasured family scrapbooks. They patiently answered my endless stream of questions, and I am grateful to them all. I thank my friend Pam Thomas, who gave me the idea for this book. I also thank the players on the Cuba Cubs team who allowed me to interview them at length: Howard Crittenden, Charles "Doodle" Floyd, Joe Buddy Warren, Jimmie Webb, Ted Bradley, Bill Pollock, and Jimmy Brown. Several of them were quite forthcoming, too, in allowing me to use photos of theirs for inclusion in this book. In that regard, I am also indebted to Donald Poyner, and to Mary Lou Floyd, Lillian Floyd Mohler, Mary Lee Story, and to Rex, Carolyn, and Barbara Story. Helen Crittenden Glover and Martha Casey Webb also provided some insights into the Cubs' childhood. I regret that I was unable to finish this book in time for Helen and Mary Lee to see it: Both died within the last two years.

I am especially grateful to Lon Carter Barton, a historian of western Kentucky and an authority on the Jackson Purchase. No one has a better understanding of the history of the Jackson Purchase and its people. Lon is a virtual human special collections library. As a member of Kentucky's house of representatives from

1958 to 1966, he acquired a keen understanding of state government politics. He provided much valuable information and often gave me support and encouragement. I also owe special thanks to Otis McPherson and his wife, Rozelle, for telling me about the history of "Little Cubie" and its inhabitants. I am thankful for Beth Page Belote and Hattie Page Glenn, who shared with me their memories of their childhood in Cuba. As children of Marion Page, for many years a Graves County physician, they had many interesting and amusing memories to share. Hattie and Beth gave me permission to read their father's journal and letters. I thank La Rue Page, Dr. Page's daughter-in-law, who unlocked the door to the doctor's old office in Cuba one crisp autumn afternoon in 1997 and kindly left me alone in it for a few minutes so that I could reflect on what might have taken place inside there a half-century ago.

Others I thank include Rachel Davis, Al McClain, Bobby McClain, Frank Wright, Barbara Harper, Pauline Harper, and Ina Warren. I appreciate librarians everywhere, and especially Debra Mayhew and her staff at Henderson County Public Library. Also, I thank our son, Chris, whose excellent computer skills solved my computer problems; our daughter, Trish, for looking after Alex, our old golden retriever, whenever her dad and I went on our frequent weekend-research jaunts; our youngest daughter, Amy, for voluntarily reading parts of early drafts and offering advice; Amy's husband, Thomas Jones, who explained and demonstrated some basketball techniques; and my young grandson, William, who also willingly read parts of the manuscript last winter and offered encouragement.

My editor, Mike Towle at Rutledge Hill Press, deserves my heartfelt thanks. Mike has been enthusiastic about the Cuba Cubs' story from the time he first saw it in the form of a proposal I sent him in 1996. With patience and encouragement, Mike shepherded me through three successive drafts.

Finally, I am thankful for my husband, Ulvester Walker, who has been my adviser, research assistant, listener, reader, and best critic. He has never once wavered in his willingness to help me.

THE CUBA CUBS
1951–52

"ALWAYS BEAR IN MIND THAT YOUR OWN RESOLUTION TO SUCCEED IS MORE IMPORTANT THAN ANY OTHER ONE THING."

—ABRAHAM LINCOLN, NOVEMBER 8, 1855,
TO ISHAM REAVIS, AN ASPIRING
LAW STUDENT

CHAPTER 1

WE SHOULDN'T HAVE LOST

"SUCCESS IS COUNTED SWEETER
BY THOSE WHO NE'ER SUCCEED."
                    —EMILY DICKINSON

Lexington, Kentucky—March 1951. It was around midnight when the bus pulled up in front of the Phoenix Hotel. A gusty wintry wind whipping around the street corner stung the faces of the teenagers as they stepped from the bus. "Man, it's cold as a well-digger's tail," one of them exclaimed as they rushed into the lobby. Instead of following the others, two tall and lanky boys, their jacket collars up around their ears and their hands thrust deeply into their pockets, turned and ambled down to the street corner, where they stopped under a lamppost. As they stood there slightly shivering while pondering what to do next, the taller of the two boys pulled a tiny silver basketball from his jeans pocket. He stared at it for a second as it gleamed in the palm of his hand under the glare of the street lamp. Then he angrily closed his fist, leaned back, lifted his arm up behind his head, and hurled the tiny ball into the black sky with all his might. As he watched it swallowed by the darkness and the whirling snow, he muttered something to himself. Then he turned his head to the side, puckered his lips, and propelled a long, dark brown ribbon of tobacco juice onto

1

the curb. The other boy, Howie, looked on with disdain and said, "Come on, Doodle, let's get to the hotel."

Even at that late hour, the lobby was noisy and crowded with people. Confetti was stuck to hats and coats; green and gold balloons floated high above heads. A few people were blowing toy horns, laughing, and talking loudly. Many others were somber, quietly bunched together in serious conversations. Bellhops carrying luggage weaved hurriedly through the crowd, stopping now and then to answer questions politely or to give directions to the "dee po." Two or three dozen elementary school-aged kids, wearing jelly-bean-colored school jackets, chased each other about the room, hollering as they trailed long ribbons of green and gold crepe paper. Some waved little green triangular pennants stamped in gold letters "Cuba Cubs," while others waved little red flags stamped in white letters "Clark County."

Howie and Doodle paused in the hotel entrance, grateful that no one noticed them. They were too tired to talk, even to each other. In three days they had played nearly every minute of four tense tournament basketball games, and they were drained emotionally and physically. To avoid the crowd waiting to board the elevators, they decided to head to the stairwell and walk up six flights of stairs to their room. Anything would be better than listen to someone tell them for the umpteenth time how great they had played and what wonderful sportsmanship they had demonstrated. Then, too, there would be the wisecrack asking for the millionth time what it was like to live in Cuba—Cuba, Kentucky.

Managing to slip past the lobby crowd without being noticed, Howie and Doodle made their way to the staircase. It was vacant and cold. A hazy streetlight pouring in through a narrow window made the marbled walls and granite steps look bluish gray. Silently and slowly, they began to limp up the stairs. Each boy was weighted down with thoughts of the recent events: the excitement of their all-day journey to Lexington in their coach's car; the marvel of visiting a big city; the strangeness of sleeping in hotel rooms and eating unfamiliar foods; the awkwardness of having to talk to people

2

they had never seen before; the embarrassment of having attention called to their "hick" western Kentucky accents and the odd name of their homeplace. On top of all those things was the indescribable thrill of playing in the Kentucky state boys' basketball tournament—something they had dreamed about doing since they were eighth graders—and the palpable joy of hearing a gymnasium filled with thousands cheering for them, the Graves County Cuba Cubs, representing the Jackson Purchase region of western Kentucky.

After climbing three flights of stairs, Howie felt weak-kneed. He propped himself up against the wall and then just slid down onto a step, saying, "Let's rest!" Doodle nodded in agreement and sat down a little way in front of him. Neither one spoke for several minutes. Then, Doodle, sitting hunched forward with his elbows on his knees and his callused brown hands cupping his face, began to sob: "Damnit! We shouldn't have lost. We shouldn't have lost." Shaking his head as he rubbed the back of his neck with both hands, he cried out again, "They shouldn't have been that much better than us." And he began pummeling the wall with his fist. His eyes were red and wet when he turned and looked up at Howie. But Howie turned away and let his head fall onto his bent arm without saying a word. He didn't want to talk about what they should have done or what they could have done. It was done. No use talking about it now.

Unlike other basketball players who were content with just playing in the state tournament, they had gone there to win. When fans congratulated them for being the runners-up, Doodle shook his head and protested sadly, "Aw, no! Being runner-up is not good enough. Near misses count only with horseshoes and hand grenades, not basketball."

Nothing could ease the boys' deep sense of loss: not the outpouring of affection that thousands showered upon them, not the honors they had received during the closing ceremonies of the tournament—Howie and Doodle were chosen to the ten-member 1951 All-State Tournament team. Jack Story, their coach, was selected Kentucky Coach of the Year. Not even the fact that all the

3

sportswriters and radio broadcasters—the same ones who at the start of the tournament had said, "Not much is expected from these mysterious underdogs"—were now saying that the Cuba Cubs "were the most popular, the most colorful, the most courageous team ever to play in the tourney." And those tiny silver basketballs engraved with "1951 Runners-Up" that the Cubs had been given, well, they were only bitter reminders of the great golden trophy that they had lost.

When Doodle and Howie got to the sixth floor of the hotel, they saw the Cuba cheerleaders standing at the other end of the hall quietly talking. The moment the girls spotted them, they ran to greet them. With tears streaming down her face, Howie's twin sister, Helen, wrapped her arms around her brother and placed her head in the crook of his neck, sobbing. Martha Casey, Barbara Harper, and Carolyn Work, all trying to be brave and cheerful, asked the boys to go with them to the party that some close fans from Cuba had planned earlier in honor of the team. It was to have been their victory party, one that Doodle and Howie had looked forward to because some girls they liked were going to attend. But now, things were different and all the boys wanted to do was sleep.

Back in their room, they were resting on the two single beds when teammates Jimmie Webb, Jimmy Jones, Joe Buddy Warren, and Raymon McClure walked in. Their glum expressions prompted Doodle to chuckle and note, in his fisherman's jargon, "Why, y'all look like red worms with all the mud slung out of them." Appearing even more dejected than the others, Joe Buddy flung his arms wide open, let them drop alongside his body, slapping his thighs, and said, "Guess what?" Looking as if he were about to cry, he added, "I left my dadgum shoes—my *Chuck Taylor All-Stars*—in Spivey's locker!" During the tournament, the Cubs had used the University of Kentucky basketball team's dressing rooms. Joe Buddy had the privilege of using Bill Spivey's locker. A great athlete, Spivey was the first seven-foot center to play for the University of Kentucky.

Raymon, who had been brooding, stopped eating the peanuts he had been snacking on, brushed the crumbs off his shirt, and

reared back in his tilted chair with his thick legs spread apart. With arms folded across his chest, he looked up and made a rude comment about Joe Buddy's "forgetfulness." The two of them began swapping some rank insults until Doodle, stretched out on his back in his underwear, with one arm lying over his eyes, shouted, "Shut up! Damnit, y'all sound like a couple of plucked hens." He rolled over in the bed, swung his long hairy legs over the side, sat up, and yawned.

Then, leaning forward, he rummaged in the back pocket of his trousers that were lying across the chair and drew out a slender book of matches, a cloth pouch of Bull Durham, and a small packet of thin white paper. Carefully, he tore off a sheet, laid it in the palm of one hand, and gently tapped out a neat little row of tobacco. Doodle was an expert at rolling cigarettes, able to fix them so that they looked like store-bought ones. As the others were waiting for Doodle to say something else, he neatly rolled the paper around the tobacco, moistened the edge of the paper with his tongue, and with a flourish, struck a match on the underside of the end table. Inhaling deeply as if he were partaking of something divine, he blew out a cloud of smoke and said, "Whew, that's good tobacco!" Then he looked around at each of them and dropped his voice to a whisper, saying, "I think we oughta quit crying about this year and figure on coming back next year and win the danged thing."

The mood suddenly brightened. As they were talking, the others on the team—Bill Pollock, Harold Roberts, Paul Simpson, Ted Bradley, Jimmy Brown—along with the student managers, Donald Poyner and Bobby McClain, entered the room. Now that they were all together, the boys began seriously talking about how they could learn from this experience. The more they talked the more upbeat their mood became. They replayed every minute of the game and pointed out where they had made mistakes. Jimmy Jones, the only senior on the team, exclaimed how lucky they were to have had this experience and for the others to have another shot at winning next year. He wished that he were a junior, too, so that he could come back with them. They agreed that the only reason they couldn't hit their shots in that final game was they were worn

5

out, plus the fact they were too timid. They admitted that they had allowed themselves to be intimidated by Clark County. But now they had a whole year to get stronger, and that's all they needed to do—get stronger and build their level of endurance.

Grinning widely, Doodle stood up, stretched, and scratched his head. He straightened his shoulders so that he towered over the rest of them. Then with his right hand spread wide open holding an imaginary basketball, he leaned to the side, stretched his long arm close to the floor, paused, and blew out a loud, long whooshing sound through his teeth as he flung the imaginary ball, pretending to make his windmill hook shot. Howie, who was always more cautious about everything than Doodle ever was, pointed out that winning the regionals again might not be as easy as making "that imaginary shot." He reminded them that they might not have to worry about Paducah Tilghman anymore—its best players would graduate that year, but they still had Ken Donaldson and Sonny Hubbs at Lone Oak to beat. "And don't forget," he added, "that Phil Rollins is still at Wickliffe." Doodle laughed faintly and said, "Oh, yeah, old Sugar Foot. Old Fantastic Phil is tough, but we can whip him and the others like him if we stick together and do what we're say we gonna do. Now, Joe Buddy, my buddy, hand me that Bible."

As they had done a few times before whenever they wanted to make a commitment, they formed a circle, put their arms around each others' shoulders, bowed their heads, and repeated an oath that Doodle, on this occasion, made up. Holding the Gideon Bible, Doodle and the boys swore to do everything they could to be better players and to get stronger physically. They swore that they were not only going to play in the '52 tournament, but they were going to win it.

"After all," Doodle concluded, widening his eyes, "ain't that what Coach Story aimed for us to do all along—win in '52?" Jimmie Webb smiled and nodded, remembering the afternoon in 1948 when he, an eighth grader, daydreaming in study hall, took out his Barlow knife and carved on the underside of his desk "Cuba Cubs—State Champions 1952."

By now, Howie was exhausted. He got back into bed, scooted under the sheets, and rolled over on his side. With his back turned to the others, he pulled the covers over his head and mumbled grumpily that he wished they'd turn out the lights and leave. As they were about to go, Coach Story popped the door open and said in a voice as dry as a cracker, "You all meet me in the front of the hotel at 7:00 A.M. sharp."

In hardly any time after the other boys had left, Howie was snoring, but Doodle was too excited to sleep. He was too happy, imagining how wonderful it would be the same time next year when the Cubs won the championship. In his mind's eye, he could see himself playing ball, scoring one bucket after another. He could hear the crowd's thunderous applause as he and the others stepped up to receive the magnificent award. He could see himself placing that gleaming trophy in the glass case in the hallway at the Cuba school. "Yessiree," he said to himself, "next year, things will be different."

In that darkened room while Howie slumbered peacefully, Doodle, dressed in his underwear, crept out of bed and danced a little jig. Then he rolled himself another cigarette and stood looking out the window, listening to the sounds of the city. The moon was shining like a new silver dollar and stars were popping out all over the sky. The lights sparkling in the city made the world look, he thought, like a precious jewel. The electric lights—the blinking lights, stoplights, neon sign lights, office building and department store lights, billboard lights—all fascinated him. Flicking a switch to turn lights off and on was as wondrous to Doodle then as was flushing the indoor toilet. Neither his nor Howie's home had electricity or running water. Nights, where they lived, were lit only with moonlight or lanterns, and the only sounds were those made by tree frogs, hounds barking in the distance, or cows moving around the pasture gently twinkling their cowbells.

On nights when there was a full moon, Howie and Doodle ran up and down the country roads near their homes. You could see their silhouettes, bathed in the silver moonlight, tossing a basketball back and forth between them.

CHAPTER 2

A GRAND
HOMECOMING

"THERE ARE SOME DEFEATS THAT ARE MORE TRIUMPHANT THAN VICTORIES."
—MONTAIGNE

Mayfield, Kentucky—1951. The next morning Howie,
Doodle, Joe Buddy, Raymon, and Jimmie Webb rode with Coach
Story as they usually did for out-of-town games. They rode in
Coach's brand-new Kaiser—a purchase that Jack Story had made
the day after the Cubs won the regionals. He was so happy that at
last he was taking his team to the state tournament in Lexington
that he splurged in buying that automobile. It was an act unchar-
acteristic of him. Without talking to his wife about his plans, he
went straight to Paducah and bought a brand-new, four-door,
two-toned, Bermuda-grass green sedan with a golden tan interior;
it matched the Cuba High School colors. He paid a little over three
thousand dollars for it, too, a big price back then.

In those days most cars were big, but the Kaiser was really big.
Unlike the secondhand Plymouth he had been driving, this car had
ample room for three adults to sit in the front and three in the back.
The manufacturers had completely redesigned the Kaiser that year,
making it less boxy, giving it more glass area and more head and leg
room. It was advertised as "the new Anatomic Design, made to fit
the human anatomy." That selling pitch may have been the very

8

thing that attracted Jack Story to this particular car. At six-foot-three and about 260 pounds, he needed a big car to drive himself and five tall, big-boned, long-legged basketball players around the state.

This car was classy looking, too, the kind that people on the sidewalk turned to look at. Its distinguishing feature was its windshield, the largest windshield of any automobile made at that time. The huge windshield header sloped down on each side and had a *V*

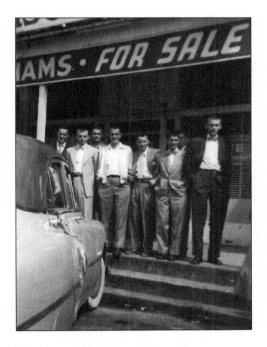

That's coach Jack Story's big and roomy Kaiser on the left, capable of accommodating five long-legged boys for out-of-town basketball trips. This photo is actually from a year later, 1952, showing the Cubs—that's Doodle Floyd on the far right—standing outside a Horse Cave lunch stop on their way back from Lexington after the 1952 state tournament. (Photo courtesy of Howie Crittenden)

in the middle, giving it the "seagull wing" appearance that became Kaiser's trademark. With its shiny K-and-buffalo badge and a dart-like mascot sitting smack dab in the center of the hood, this car was the grandest thing that Coach Story and the Cubs had ever seen and riding in it made them feel special—like world-class winners.

Young Joe McPherson, assistant coach and history teacher, drove the other five players home in his four-door blue Ford, while Jess Warren, Joe Buddy's dad, filled his car with others involved with the team. Some of the cheerleaders and team managers followed in cars driven by Robert Wagoner and Jack Olive, young men from Pilot Oak. Folks from Cuba and the Jackson Purchase made up the remainder of the motorcade, thirty-five or forty automobiles.

Lexington is about 270 miles from Mayfield and, back then, the drive took the better part of a day. There were no modern interstates for them to travel on, only two-lane roads winding through one small town after another. The highway speed limit was fifty or fifty-five miles an hour. Having to stop in every town and hamlet for stoplights, stop signs or intersections, railroad and cattle crossings made the ride even slower.

The farther they traveled along U.S. 62 out of Lexington, the more people they saw standing along the roadside waving to them. When Coach Story pulled to a stop in front of the Horse Cave Cafe, where he had earlier made arrangements for them to eat lunch, the string of cars following him also stopped. A hundred or so people stood on either side of the street in front of the cafe, waiting to welcome them that cold, overcast day.

It seems that after Coach Story had made the luncheon reservation, the cafe owner—thrilled to have such celebrities in his establishment—called friends from all over Edmonson County to come to Horse Cave to meet the Coach of the Year and his Cuba Cubs. Hardly anybody got much to eat that day because of all the excitement in and around the cafe.

A little west of Horse Cave, at Bowling Green, the motorcade got on Kentucky 80, which led them into Mayfield. As they traveled

10

through each town—Bowling Green, Rockfield, Auburn, Russell-
ville, Elktown, Hopkinsville, Cadiz, Canton, Golden Pond, and Aurora—they were met by another sheriff or constable who would
then lead them through the town. Onlookers parked in cars on either side of the narrow main streets started blowing their horns
once they spotted the sheriff or the constable leading the green
Kaiser. To them, Cuba represented the dreams of all tiny communities across the great state of Kentucky—the Cubs' success was theirs,
too. Stretched across plain wooden storefronts were wide paper
banners proclaiming, "Welcome, Cuba Cubs!" Adults and children
stood on the sidewalks, alongside the roads, or in front of houses,
law offices, hardware stores, and other businesses, waving pennants
and flags and yelling, "Yea! Cuba!" Dogs ran barking alongside the
Kaiser as the Cubs' long, outstretched arms waved from the car windows. In some town squares, little high school bands played "Sweet
Georgia Brown," the Cubs' theme song.

This seemingly endless gauntlet of enthusiastic well-wishers
was the result of the efforts of a small group in Horse Cave, who
had initiated a network of telephone calls. The residents of one town
would ring people in the next town to alert them that the motorcade was headed their way. This network ultimately stretched 140
miles from Horse Cave to Eggner's Ferry Bridge in Aurora, in the
far western end of the state. No one, no place, seemed to mind that
the Cubs were only the runners-up. The people loved the way the
Cubs played ball—with speed, accuracy, and showmanship. All
across Kentucky there was talk about Howie's magical ball handling
and Doodle's phenomenal hook shot.

At Pete Light Springs, east of Kentucky Lake, several hundred
people waited. Parked along the highway was a train of bright, new,
crayola-colored Cadillac convertibles for the Cubs to transfer into
for the last stretch of their ride to Mayfield. The cars had been provided by Mayfield and Paducah automobile dealers who had gone
as far as Nashville to get enough open-tops to take the players,
coaches, cheerleaders, team managers, and anyone else in the
junior class who had anything to do with the team.

Carrying the handsome runners-up trophy, Coach Story, Howie, Joe Buddy, and Ted were seated in the first Cadillac, a sparkling gold-tinted convertible with a dark green interior, driven by Franklin Cleaver, a youth from Cuba. The other starters, reserves, and managers got into the following convertibles. With a Kentucky state patrol car leading the way, the motorcade crept homeward to Graves County.

When they reached Eggner's Ferry Bridge on the Marshall County border about 4:15 that cold, cloudy afternoon, Coach Story and the Cubs stared in disbelief. Some five hundred automobiles were parked near the bridge, and a crowd estimated at a thousand cheered as the Cubs drew close. All those who did not have the money to go to the tournament, or who could not leave work, or sick or elderly folks or farm animals unattended came to the Eggner's Ferry Bridge to welcome the Cubs home. After greetings were exchanged, a couple of state troopers led the five-hundred-car motorcade across Marshall County and into Graves County to Mayfield. The convoy was so long that by the time the lead automobile got to Hardin, the last car was just leaving the bridge area. By now, the motorcade was eight miles long.

None of the Cubs or Jack Story could sit still or face forward in the convertibles. All kept turning their heads and craning their necks to look back at the train of cars snaking behind for as far as they could see. All along the route children and adults stood in their front yards along the highway, shouting and waving to the Cubs.

Twilight had fallen by the time they crossed the Graves County line. When they arrived at the courthouse square in Mayfield, they were astonished to find a crowd that newspapers the next day estimated at eight thousand. The courthouse square had been packed for more than an hour and no parking space could be found within six blocks. The crowd cheered as Coach Story and the Cubs got out of the convertibles, shaking as many of the outstretched hands as they could reach as they headed toward the platform, where a public-address system had been set up and city and county officials and western Kentucky politicians had gathered.

It was a cold crisp evening. A gentle wind stirred the green and gold crepe paper and banners decorating the platform. A large U.S. flag and an equally large Cuba school flag, prominently displayed near the podium, waved softly. The Mayfield High School band, outfitted in fire-engine red uniforms, snappily paraded up to the platform where they played "America the Beautiful," "The Star-Spangled Banner," and the Cuba school song, while the crowd sang along. When Coach Story and the Cubs filed onto the platform and the band burst into "Sweet Georgia Brown," the Cubs' theme song, everybody went wild.

Getting his audience to settle down so he could begin the ceremony was not easy for the master of ceremonies, Bob Butterworth, president of the Mayfield-Graves County Chamber of Commerce. Finally, he was able to introduce the mayor, Scott Lemon; the state senator, Wayne Freeman; the state representative, L. M. T. Reed; the commonwealth attorney, F. B. Martin; the county attorney, Lucien Smith; and the two most powerful political figures in the county: William Foster, president of Merit Clothing Company, and Ed Gardner, president of the First National Bank. After they each said a few words, he introduced C. T. Winslow, president of the Kiwanis Club, who spoke on behalf of all the civic clubs in the county. Next the superintendent of Graves County schools, James B. "Baby" DeWeese, led the Pledge of Allegiance and offered his welcome and congratulations. He was followed by Cuba cheerleader Joyce Breedlove and Cuba team manager Bobby McClain. No one remembers a word of any of the speeches because of what immediately followed Bobby's talk when the microphone was handed to Coach Story. Coach Story was so choked up that he was unable to speak or even look at the audience. With his head bowed and his chin resting on his chest, he stood silently staring at the floor as he struggled to gain his composure. After an embarrassingly long silence, he looked up and around at the crowd and then said simply, "Thank you. Thank you. You're the grandest people in the world."

Trying to break the emotional tension, the master of ceremonies asked the Cubs to stand up so that he could introduce each of them. The boys rose, scraping their chairs back nervously. They looked handsome, dressed in dark topcoats, suits, white shirts, ties, and leather shoes—outfits that the merchants from the Mayfield men's clothing stores had given them before they left for Lexington. Unable to stay still, Doodle leaned closer to Howie and whispered, "I feel like I've got a lump in my throat big enough to choke a cow." He no more got those words out when the mayor thrust the microphone into his face.

"Well, Charles Floyd, what does it feel like to be a member of the All-State team?"

Wide-eyed, the boy stammered, "Well, sir, I was skeered during the tournament, and I'm skeered now. All I got really to say is I'm sorry, real sorry, we lost. But I promise we won't let you down next year." The crowd erupted into laughter and cheers.

Turning away from the audience and looking directly at Coach Story, Doodle blurted out, "We goin' back next year, Coach. Next year, we're gonna get that championship trophy."

Unexpectedly, Joe Buddy popped up, grabbed the microphone, and shouted, "Yes, sir, we're going back. Why, I left my Chuck Taylors in Spivey's locker, and I want them back, too!" The crowd roared with laughter and broke out in thunderous applause.

When the band started playing "Sweet Georgia Brown" again, the cheerleaders shed their overcoats and hopped up onto the platform. They clapped and jumped up and down to the music. Then they started shouting, "Cuba! Cuba! Yes, it's true—State Cham-p-ion in '52!" The crowd picked up the chant and went on and on with it for the longest time. The master of ceremonies tried to continue the program but to no avail. His audience had heard all it wanted to hear.

CHAPTER 3

THE LAND BETWEEN THE RIVERS

"MEN'S CUSTOMS DIFFER; DIFFERENT PEOPLE HONOR DIFFERENT PRACTICES;
BUT ALL HONOR THE MAINTENANCE OF THEIR OWN PECULIAR WAYS."
—PLUTARCH

Jackson Purchase—1818–1951. The phenomenal support that Cuba, Graves County, and the rest of the Jackson Purchase gave to Coach Story and his Cubs did not go unnoticed elsewhere in the state. Across the commonwealth newspapers featured photographs and articles about the coach, the team, and the incredible reception. They carried aerial photographs of the automobiles parked near Eggner's Ferry Bridge, of the eight-mile-long motorcade to Mayfield, and of the celebration at the county courthouse square.

In one of his columns summarizing the tournament, *Lexington Herald-Leader* veteran sportswriter Bob Adair compared the western Kentucky spirit to "the local spirit" and wondered why "the local spirit" was so lacking. He wrote, "Central Kentuckians can sit by the fireside or find other recreation during the district and regional play, and then complain for lack of tickets when the classic rolls around." Not so with the Cuba fans. From the beginning of the basketball season to the end, they packed every gym in which the Cubs played. In the small rural schools, the gyms would be so crowded that the corners of the court would be rounded off.

Adair pointed out: "Cuba, population one hundred, or there-abouts, was literally evacuated when the Cubs came to Lexington and brought everyone within a radius of many miles with them. Those fans had to travel some three hundred miles. Yet a very small percentage of the people of Lexington took the trouble to ride across town and root for Henry Clay. And a very small percentage of those who took the trouble to ride across town rooted for the Blue Devils. In fact, counting those who did attend, the Demons had very little backing other than in the school's own cheering section, which prob-ably was second-best only to Manual's large contingent." He went on to write about "the embarrassment suffered when townspeople hurled insults at the Blue Devils and the officials while clamoring and raving for Cuba."

No one ever found a Cuba supporter even whispering an in-sult about its players or officials, much less hurling or spewing one at them. You could go to the bank with your money on a bet that no basketball fan in western Kentucky would ever root for any team other than their own—under any circumstances. Western Kentuckians, the reporter concluded, are uniquely unified in their commitment to their teams.

In 1951 hardly anyone in central Kentucky—the cultural, po-litical, and academic center of the state—had ever heard of the tiny place named Cuba or, for that matter, knew anything about the Jackson Purchase, a peninsula-looking strip of land jutting out of west Tennessee into the far western tip of Kentucky. Surrounded by rivers on three sides, the Purchase was born in 1818, when Kentucky was already twenty-five years old. For a hundred years the state went on about its business as if the new section had not even been added to it. Until the late 1930s the political powers in Frankfort largely ignored the region because finding anything other than a registered Democrat in the Purchase was like finding hair on a frog's head. The Purchase still is a Democratic strong-hold, but not to the extent it was in the past. With a few excep-tions, the Democrats have always had control of the state government. Whenever they had control or were seeking control, they never bothered wooing the Purchase because they saw no advantage in spending their money in an area that they knew they would carry in any election anyway. On the other hand, the Republicans never sought the Purchase's favor either, figuring they would be wasting their money.

Until the late 1930s and early 1940s, the state politicians, for the most part, directed no funds toward building roads, schools, bridges, or state office buildings in the Purchase, nor did they set up the multitude of semilocal agencies that are part of a state government. For example, Graves County in the late 1940s was given an agricultural extension agency but no laboratories or facilities. However, the agency in nearby Hopkins County, which is in western Kentucky but not in the Purchase, had a first-class operation. Just as it is today, politicians preferred spending state and federal money in those counties having balanced party systems. Politically speaking, you can say that the Purchase disadvantaged itself by adhering so strictly to its Democratic stand. Throughout the state not much was known about the region, and that's why the newspaper articles about the Cubs at the start of the tournament differed from the ones at the end when the *Louisville Courier-Journal* felt obliged to produce an article about Cuba and the Jackson Purchase.

When the Cubs first arrived in Lexington, newscasters were asking, "Cuba? Who's Cuba? Where's Cuba?" They knew about the larger western Kentucky teams like Paducah Tilghman and Owensboro Senior High, and the smaller ones like Brewers, Wickliffe, and Lone Oak. They considered Tilghman the best in the western Kentucky region. Having never heard of the Cuba Cubs, they described them as, among other things, "the little crossroads team," "the Cinderella team," and "the Unknowns . . . the mysterious underdogs." One headline hailed them as "the Enigma."

A few disrespectful critics called them "hot-doggity hicks" and joked, "Here come the Cubans! Hah! Hah! The hillbilly ones! Hah! Hah!" Others, with warmhearted humor, teased them about their speech patterns and their "Cuban suntans." The Cubs' hands, wrists, backs of their necks, and their faces, except for that part which had been protected by hats, were much darker than the rest of their bodies. Years of living most of their lives outdoors, working in tobacco patches and on farms, had permanently darkened the exposed parts of their bodies.

The word *hillbilly* did not accurately describe the Cubs, nor did it stick to them long once they were seen playing on the hardwood. Among those they won over with their grace and precision was Kentucky governor Lawrence Wetherby. Shortly before the final tournament game was to begin, Governor Wetherby spoke at a Lexington Chamber of Commerce party held for all those involved with the tournament. In a startling announcement described in the newspapers as "speaking undiplomatically," Governor Wetherby stated, "I'm for Cuba, all the way. The way those kids fight, and just don't want to lose, makes sports great. So you take Manual, Clark County, and the rest. I'll just be for those kids from Cuba."

The governor and others recognized that the difference between the Cubs and their more cosmopolitan contemporaries was not just in their manners and speech or in the way they played ball, but in a much deeper sense. The Cubs had a kind of Old-World, frontier-spirit ruggedness about them that was distinctive and admirable. The way they persisted and the way they functioned as a team—like nimble fingers on a deft right hand—reflected their pioneer background. Cuba was not a deep team and couldn't substitute as efficiently as the large schools could. Despite their injuries or illnesses, Cuba's starters played nearly every minute of every Cuba game unless, of course, they fouled out—but they knew better than to do that.

To many of the more sophisticated in the Blue Grass region, the Cubs could not avoid appearing quaint and countrified. Their temperament and style had been shaped by the Jackson Purchase where life in 1951 in many respects more closely resembled that in the late nineteenth century. More of the old ways persisted in the Purchase because three forbidding rivers for so long had geographically kept it apart from the mainstream political and social centers. Like giant arms, the Ohio River on the north, the Mississippi on the west, and the Tennessee on the east side wrap around the Purchase, cutting it entirely off from Kentucky and from other land, except on the south side where the Purchase joins Tennessee. In the early stages of its history, the Purchase couldn't build wagon bridges over any of the rivers because of their great width and water-level fluctuations, and so its people grew accustomed to staying within their own borders. One generation after another placed great value on tradition. They didn't see anything wrong with continuing some practices in pretty much the same style as their ancestors.

From 1818 to 1905, no bridges were built over any of the rivers. Then the Illinois Central Railroad Company built a locomotive bridge over the Tennessee River at Gilbertsville so that passengers could ride the train between Louisville and Memphis. But no vehicular bridges were built over any of the rivers for over a hundred years because no state and federal funds for such construction had been allocated. The first vehicular bridge—the Irvin S. Cobb Bridge—was built in 1929. Stretching across the Ohio River, it connected Paducah, the largest city in the Purchase, to Bridgeport, Illinois. Ferries transporting people and freight over the other rivers were inconvenient or too expensive to use often. Just getting to the ferries was difficult enough because many roads were not paved or even graveled until the late 1940s.

For the most part, the Purchase people had no real interest in crossing those rivers. Having been ignored for so long by the state's political powers, they felt no real attachment to Kentucky, even after the state began to show them some attention. Their kinship was with Tennessee. Even after the Eggner's Ferry Bridge across the Tennessee River at Aurora was completed in 1933, finally linking the Purchase to the rest of Kentucky, few took advantage of it.

The Purchase is part of the territory which Andrew Jackson of Tennessee and Isaac Shelby, twice governor of Kentucky, purchased from the Chickasaw Nation in 1818. The largest portion of that eight thousand square miles east of the Mississippi River and north of the Mississippi state line went to Tennessee and is called West Tennessee; the smaller part went to Kentucky and is named after Jackson.

Ancestors of Jack Story and the Cubs were among those pioneers who came to the Purchase in the 1830s. These settlers were common people, escaping hard economic times in the Carolinas, Virginia, middle Tennessee, and central Kentucky. Some historians claim that the personality and temperament of Purchase people is just like that of Jackson, who was called Old Hickory because he was tough as hickory wood. Tenacious and self-reliant almost to a fault, Jackson succeeded sometimes on nothing but sheer willpower. Coach Story used him as a model for teaching the Cubs not to give up and not to make too much of their pain—ever. A stoic himself, Story told the boys about Jackson, "a real soldier," who—without any anesthetic—sat in a chair and leaned on his cane while a surgeon carved a bullet out of his shoulder.

The descendants of the southerners who settled the Jackson Purchase maintained the old southern code of honor—an ethic that emphasized loyalty to homeplace and family, not the Union or the state. What Lexington sportswriter Bob Adair and others claimed was a remarkable display of unified support, loyalty, and pride was simply a reflection of regional distinction. Purchase people had a deep sense of place and an independent spirit. They were a nation unto themselves—"independent as a hawg on ice!"

They were so independent that when Kentucky declared its neutrality in 1861, just after the Civil War started, many of them wanted to separate from Kentucky and unite with West Tennessee to form a new Confederate state. Although this proposal was defeated, more than six thousand Purchase men joined the Confederate military, while fewer than six hundred went to the Union forces. The Purchase paid dearly for being such a Confederate stronghold. Before the war it had been a flourishing district of farmers shipping tons of dark-fired tobacco, smoked hams, bacon, lard, cotton, and wheat down the Mississippi River to market in New Orleans. After the war, the Purchase was broke.

Its people grew accustomed to hardships and were oftentimes ignorant of the opportunities offered in the outside world. They were attached to their homes and families and to a simple way of life. They brought their children up the same way they had been reared. Their children and many of their children's children lived and died in the communities into which they had been born without ever having moved away.

When the Cubs' parents were young farmers in the 1920s and 1930s, they had a hard time making a living. That was even before the Great Depression hit in 1933—the year most of the Cubs were born—when farming fell into an even steeper decline. Although the national economy improved in 1935 and 1936, it bottomed out suddenly in the summer of 1937, and the country spiraled down into a recession. Lacking electric power, rural areas had no industries to provide jobs, until the Tennessee Valley Authority started building dams across the rivers in the late 1930s. Many farmers, like Howie's and Doodle's dads and Coach Story, left the Purchase for a few years to work in northern factories. Michigan, especially, became a mecca for poor Kentuckians.

Finally, the Jackson Purchase began to gain some economic stability in the mid-1950s, when electric power was supplied to all the rural areas. A little later, dams, bridges, roads, the Purchase Parkway, and Interstate 24 were built, thoroughly connecting the region with the rest of the world. Even then, as late as 1951, when Jack Story and his Cuba Cubs went to Lexington for the state tournament, much of the Purchase was still backward—socially, technologically, and economically. Not to say that it was Dogpatch, populated with benighted hillbillies. It produced a good share of prominent citizens, among them Julian Carroll, governor of Kentucky; Nathan B. Stubblefield, inventor of the wireless telephones (forerunner of the radio); and Thomas Scopes of the Scopes Monkey Trial fame. The most famous of all, and the greatest inspiration for the Cuba Cubs, was Alben William Barkley, the thirty-fifth vice president of the United States. Born in 1877 in Graves County, he was reared in a log cabin, near Lowes, only twenty-four miles from Cuba. Just like Howie and Doodle, Barkley was the son of a tenant farmer who wrung a scant living from the ground raising dark-fired tobacco.

21

MILKING, MOWING, SUCKERIN' TOBACCO, AND PLAYING BALL

"ENDURE AND PERSIST; THIS PAIN WILL TURN TO YOUR GOOD BY AND BY."
—OVID

Graves County—1933–1948. The Cubs did not all know each other while they were growing up. None of them was born in Cuba, a hamlet with a population of 150 or so, but all were from southern Graves County.

Joe Buddy Warren was born in Lynn Grove where his father, Jess, started out as a sharecropper on the Effie Morris farm. When Joe Buddy was around six, Jess bought a house and a sixty-five-acre farm in Cuba. He farmed until World War II started, and then he went into the service. His wife, Ina, went to work at the new ammunition plant in Viola, outside of Mayfield. After the war Jess farmed and worked some at the school for Coach Story. Ina worked at the Merit Clothing Company in Mayfield. They were one of the few families in Cuba who always had a car and usually it would be a fairly new one. Jess was one of the few farmers who had a tractor. Until he left home with an athletic scholarship to Murray State Teachers College, now Murray State University, Joe Buddy lived with his parents and his sister in a house on the main road, about a half-mile from the Cuba school.

Joe Buddy entered the first grade at the school in Cuba along with a few others who became part of the Cubs' team. The head student manager for the team was Donald Poyner, a small thin boy who loved sports, especially baseball. But Cuba did not have a baseball team while he was growing up. Although he did not play basketball, Donald was Coach Story's right-hand man, and he had a role in the team's success. The youngest and perhaps the brightest in his class, Donald went on to become valedictorian. He was born in 1934 in Fairbanks, where his parents, Em Boyd and Clara, operated a small grocery store until 1940, when they moved to Cuba. They lived on the main road, across the street from the Warrens.

The two other student managers, Mason Harris and Bobby McClain, lived with their parents on farms just outside Cuba. Al McClain, who was distantly related to Bobby, was also in their class but was never on the team. He preferred working at the Mayfield radio station in his spare time and went on to become a news and sports broadcaster. Aught, his dad, was a sharecropper and also the only barber in Cuba. Every Friday for years Aught cut hair in the back room at Rhodes General Store. Raymon McClure, one of the Cubs' most aggressive rebounders, was strong as a bull even when he was in grade school. Raymon lived about two miles from Cuba on the road going toward Sedalia. Others who were reserves on the team were Paul Simpson, Harold Roberts, Jimmy Lowery, and Jimmy Brown. All lived on farms between Cuba and Mayfield. Ted Bradley, usually the first off the bench to replace Joe Buddy, moved from Fulton to Cuba when he was in the fourth grade. From then on, he and Joe Buddy were great friends. They hunted and fished together. Ted's dad farmed and worked in Mayfield part-time as a sign painter. Although Duane Hill did not play on the varsity, he was a starter on the junior varsity. Duane's left arm was shot off in a hunting accident when he was around ten, but he learned to play basketball amazingly well with one arm. All of these boys played basketball together during recess and the lunch break.

Another starter and great set shot was Jimmie Webb, who lived on a farm halfway between Cuba and Pilot Oak, about five miles from the school in Cuba. Back then, whenever half a dozen families settled in the same area, someone would open a store, and the area would be named after the store. So Jimmie Webb lived in Wrays, near Wray's General Store. An only child, he helped his father on their sixty-acre farm. They raised tobacco and milked ten cows by hand. His dad worked the night shift at the Pet Milk factory in Mayfield. His mother's first cousins, Carl and Fred Rhodes, owned Rhodes's, one of the two general stores in Cuba. His grandparents lived in Cuba across the field from the school, and Jimmie used to spend a lot of nights with them after ball games. They never saw any of the Cubs' games, but they listened to them on the radio. Until he was in the sixth grade, Jimmie attended school in Pilot Oak with Howie and Doodle, who were both born in Pilot Oak, eight miles southwest of Cuba, close to the Tennessee state line.

Life in southern Graves County was lean and hard and isolated. The one cash crop was dark-fired tobacco; everybody raised it. Graves County was, and still is, one of the world's largest producers of dark-fired tobacco. There were few cars, no electricity, and no running water. There were no picture shows, drive-ins, or television. There were a few battery-operated, party-line telephones, and an occasional radio picked up static-shredded broadcasts from the outside world—ball games, boxing matches, caterwauling preachers, country music. Mostly, there was a lot of time and a lot of outdoors.

The daily rhythm of life was the same in each of the Cub's homes. By 4:30 in the morning, everyone was up and about, including the children old enough to work. After trips to the outhouse, everyone got dressed and went about doing his or her chores. The hogs and chickens had to be fed and the cows milked, often by the light of a handheld lantern. Water had to be drawn from the cistern, milk brought in from the cowshed, eggs gathered from the hen house, sausage and bacon carried in from the smokehouse. Only then could breakfast be started.

Before breakfast could be cooked, however, the wood stove in the kitchen had to be fired up. That was done by first going out to the corn bin, filling a five-gallon coal bucket with corn cobs, dipping one cob into some coal oil, placing it in the bottom of the fire box in the stove, and piling the others on top of it. As the fire started building, coal or kindling wood was added to it. The fire had to be watched so that it didn't go out or get too hot. The soot pan and the ash box, under the stove, had to be kept clean, or the stove wouldn't work right. Usually, the sons in a family would take turns keeping those pans clean and splitting wood for the stove. Occasionally, those duties were assigned as punishments for boys, like Doodle, who often misbehaved.

The stove generally had four or six burners, called eyes, and a griddle for cooking pancakes, sausage, and bacon. Two warming closets above the cooking surface kept food warm until it was served. Off to the right side of the stove was a baking oven. The trick to baking cakes and biscuits was to start them in the lower part of the oven, where they browned quickly, and then move them up to the top section to bake slowly. Cooking and baking on a wood stove was no easy task because the heat could not be regulated. The cook had to watch what she was doing. She had to keep turning the food, moving the pan around off and on the eye.

Before breakfast the feather pillows and the straw mattresses had to be shaken out and all the beds made. Mattresses were handmade and filled with straw or sometimes corn shucks. Every spring the stuffing was replaced with fresh straw. The pillows were made with feathers plucked from the breasts of ducks, geese, and chickens. As the youngest in his family, Doodle had the job of catching the duck or the goose and holding its wings, while his sister Lillian plucked the feathers and stuffed them in a sack. The birds vigorously objected to this process, which had to be repeated many times before enough feathers were collected to make a feather pillow. Doodle dreaded his role. If he accidentally let one of the birds go before Lillian, his older sister, finished with it, she'd spank him. She was like a second mother, only stricter than their mother.

Breakfast consisted of boiled coffee, biscuits, eggs, potatoes or pancakes, sausage or bacon, and milk gravy made in the black cast-iron skillet that the meat had been fried in. The hot milk gravy was poured over the hot biscuits, although some preferred molasses over their biscuits, so a jar of it was kept on the table. After breakfast any leftover food was covered with a clean towel and left on the back of the stove to be eaten later; nothing was wasted. The floor was swept with a broom handmade from twigs; and the pots and dishes were washed and put away. If school were in session, the children would run to catch the school bus. If it were not, they would go about doing their chores.

After breakfast the men vanished into the barns and fields, and the women went about their work—cooking, cleaning, sewing, canning, and gardening. Every family had a large garden for growing vegetables and fruits that were dried, stored, or preserved to feed the family all winter. The women seldom worked in the fields but tended the vegetable gardens with the help of younger children, and they gathered wildflowers, herbs, and blackberries growing abundantly beside the roads and throughout unplowed fields. Herbs were gathered for cooking and medicinal purposes and the berries for desserts and preserves.

In the summer baths were taken outside, where the sun warmed the water in the large galvanized tubs. In the winter the tubs were set in the kitchen, the warmest room in the house. Clothes were washed outside in huge kettles, with water hauled from the cistern and boiled over a wood fire. Most people didn't own enough clothes to put clean ones on every day, and by the end of the week, overalls were hard to scrub clean.

After they had done their chores, children were free to roam. They felt at home no matter where they were. No Trespassing signs did not exist. They swam and fished in the ponds; picked blackberries, walnuts, and pecans; and hunted coons, birds, squirrels, and rabbits wherever they pleased. Some played basketball on the dirt courts in front of the stores. Each store owner kept a basketball under the counter for whoever wanted it. In those days a basketball—a good one, at least—was not something that every boy owned. But every stable, tobacco barn, milk house, or outbuilding had some kind of basketball goal, usually a makeshift one made from an old barrel rim or bicycle wheel. If they didn't have a ball, they made one out of rags or they used tin cans for balls.

One great thing about basketball is that a player does not need expensive equipment or someone to practice with. He can practice all he wants, whenever he wants, and for as long as he wants, all by himself. Some Pilot Oak residents can still remember Howie Crittenden practicing his dribbling, oftentimes in the dark, on a blacktop road between Pilot Oak and Water Valley. Occasionally, he would dribble four or five miles in a session. He and Doodle Floyd often ran the eight miles to and from Cuba, dribbling and passing the ball between them. It was a Kentucky basketball version of a fast-break marathon.

The school in Cuba housed grades one through twelve, as was customary for rural schools in those days. (Photo courtesy of Donald Poyner)

27

Back then nearly all of the rural county schools in Kentucky housed grades one through twelve and were simply named after the community in which they existed. Most of the schools were two-storied, wooden-framed buildings that had no running water or electricity. Few had gymnasiums, and those gymnasiums were not sized according to regulations. Any school with twelve grades was called a "high school," indicating that a high school diploma could be earned there. If a grade-school-age child said he went to Cuba or to Pilot Oak, everyone knew what school he was talking about. There was no such institution as a Cuba Middle or Elementary School, or, say, a Lynn Grove Junior High.

Because the economy in Kentucky had been so bad for so long, many rural Kentuckians by the late 1930s had moved north to find work. Consequently, the enrollment in all the rural schools was low. Then, too, many youths thought by the time they had completed the sixth or seventh grade that they had all the education they'd ever need. Attendance varied in all the schools. During 1946–47 the state department of education began closing grades seven or eight through twelve in places that had low enrollment and began busing students to one central location. This change occurred just as the Cubs were ready to enter the eighth grade, so the ones who were not already attending the Cuba school had to transfer there. It was that twist of fate that brought them all together for the first time.

CHAPTER 5

DOODLE FLOYD

"A BOY'S WILL IS THE WIND'S WILL, AND THOUGHTS OF YOUTH ARE LONG,
LONG THOUGHTS."
    —HENRY WADSWORTH LONGFELLOW

Pilot Oak, Kentucky—1933–1948. When they were both nine
years old, Howie and Doodle forged a friendship that endured
throughout their lives. Even though they were kindred spirits, they
were an odd match. Small and thin for his age, with butternut dark
gold hair, Howie was a quiet boy, polite and intense. He was a serious student. Doodle was taller, heavier, big-boned, and physically
strong for his age. He was a gregarious, friendly, good-natured child.
Because of his warm spontaneity for fun, everyone who knew Doodle loved him. Unlike Howie, he was not a good student. He did not
like to read nor take time to do homework. School, for him, was
more of a social center, a place to see his friends and to play basketball. Beneath these differences, the two boys had a common and
abiding love of play and competition. Local residents became accustomed to seeing the boys together, engaged in games that were really
one long continuous competition, extended from season to season.

From the time he was six until he graduated from high school
in 1952, Doodle lived with his family on a forty-five-acre farm, a little over three miles from Pilot Oak. The farm was just off the Pilot
Oak-Dukedom road, close to the Tennessee state line. His dad had
paid eight hundred dollars in cash for the property, using money he

had earned as a carpenter millwright setting machines and turbines in Detroit, where he worked three to four months every winter for years. The rest of the year he worked in Pilot Oak as a sharecropper.

Until he bought his own land, Doodle's father worked on the Johnny Morris farm. The house that Mr. Morris provided for the Floyds and their seven children was no more than a small backwoods shack on the Wingo road, about half a mile out of Pilot Oak. Weatherboarded on the outside, it had a tin roof, three tiny rooms, and three windows. Doodle was born in this house on April 23, 1933, the last of the six sons born to Lexie Belle Jackson and Vodie Carnell Floyd. A year younger than her husband, Lexie was thirty-seven years old when Doodle was born.

Christened Charles Kenneth Floyd, Doodle got his nickname when he was about four, when his dad teased him about playing with doodle bugs. Doodle entered this world as a main attraction, weighing nearly fifteen pounds. Neighbors who came to see him the day of his birth said he looked like a three-month-old child. Old Dr. Bard, from Wingo, said Doodle was the biggest baby he had ever *caught* (a term country doctors used for the word *deliver*). All the Floyds were well over six feet tall—big-boned, lean, and strong—so Doodle's size really was no great surprise.

His five older brothers were Herschel, Harold, William, Hobert, and James, who was three years old when Doodle was born. Harold had died of blood poisoning in 1927 at ten years of age, six years before Doodle was born. Lillian Beatrice, the only daughter, was thirteen years older than Doodle, and she looked after him and James. Even as a child, she worked hard helping her mother. From the time she was seven until she left home at sixteen, Lillian missed school every Monday to help her mother wash clothes.

Until he was a junior in high school, Doodle wore old clothes and shoes passed down from his brothers. Once a year everyone in the family got a new pair of shoes, but they could be worn only at school and church. At all other times the children wore whatever shoes that the older ones had outgrown. Most of the time, the small children went barefoot, unless it was too wet or cold.

(Left to right) Hobert Floyd, age fifteen, and James Floyd, twelve, are joined by younger brother Doodle, nine, standing in front of the Model A Ford just bought by their father, Vodie. He bought the car in Detroit, but somebody else drove it back to Kentucky for him because he hadn't yet learned how to drive. (Photo courtesy of Charles Floyd)

When Doodle was about three, his father and John Morris, the landowner, had an argument over the crop division, and Mr. Morris fired Vodie. Apparently, Mr. Morris thought that Vodie had cheated him, even though it was generally known that that wasn't the case. Vodie Floyd was honest and hardworking. The argument was unpleasant and humiliating, but sharecroppers were often the subject of humiliation. With seven children and a wife to feed, Vodie took the first job offered to him. He went to work on the old Roland place, near Water Valley, where conditions were better and the house much nicer.

31

The Floyds lived on the Roland farm until 1939, when they bought their own place: forty-five acres that had a dilapidated house, an old tobacco barn, a hen house, an outhouse, and a smokehouse. Actually, the smokehouse, with its dirt floor, was in better shape than the main house, which was built with rough barn-wood boards running perpendicular to the ground. Had the boards been nailed overlapping each other horizontally, the outside walls of the house would have been much tighter. As it was, the boards with their uneven edges were butted against each other and narrow planks were nailed over the seams in an attempt to keep out the cold. Because there were no interior walls, Vodie used pieces of cardboard and anything else he could find to cover the cracks in the planks that inevitably appeared with changes in the temperature. Nevertheless, the rain and snow still blew in during storms. The house had three rooms, four screenless windows, and a back porch that Vodie enclosed with weatherboarding. After a year or so, Lexie and Lillian covered the walls with heavy gray paper, using paste they made from flour and water. This wallpaper not only made the rooms look a little better but helped keep out the cold.

Lexie and Vodie slept in the living room, and the older boys shared the two double beds in the other bedroom. Until she married at sixteen and moved away, Lillian slept on a cot alongside Doodle, a baby, on the closed-in porch.

Their kitchen consisted of an old cast-iron, wood-burning stove; one open cabinet filled with white dishes and crockery, another with pots and pans; a small table with a pan used for washing dishes; and a long table with two benches that Vodie had made out of oak. Lexie cooked on the wood-burning stove and baked meals for her large family. She also canned fruits and vegetables. During the summers she made strawberry, peach, gooseberry, and blackberry pies and jam. She was a marvelous cook and served scrumptious meals in her humble way. She baked biscuits on the lids of five-gallon lard cans. Because her family liked biscuits hot, she'd always have a lid loaded with freshly made ones ready to pop into the

Doodle's mom, Lexie, was a hardworking farmer's wife.
(Photo courtesy of Charles Floyd)

stove. Until the children moved away, the family sat down at the table together for three meals a day. Vodie always said the blessing before a morsel was eaten.

They never had beef, and Doodle never tasted any until he was grown. Every winter, his parents butchered hogs, using every part except "the squeal." They used the "middlin'" for bacon, the head for souse, and the feet for pickling. The rest was made up of hams, chops, ribs, and roasts. The "scraps, liver, and lights (lungs)" were ground up, seasoned, packed in a muslin sack or a clean, old sleeve cut from a shirt, and smoked with the hams in the smokehouse. All the meat was first packed in salt and later smoked by a slow, smoldering hickory-wood fire for several days. All of it was kept in the smokehouse year round. Even the scrap hog fat was saved and added to Merrywar Lye to make soap.

After all the work was done on hog-killing day, the women prepared a huge meal for the workers. A gentle child, James could never participate in the hog-killing activities. He dreaded the event, while others considered it a kind of celebration.

Early on, Doodle got the idea of how wonderful it was to excel in sports. He, his dad, and James listened to the boxing matches on the radio. They walked by lantern light to Jess Erington's house two miles away to listen to special events on Jess's radio. They all especially admired boxer Joe Louis, who dominated the heavyweight division from 1937 to 1949. On their walks to and from Jess's house, Vodie would hold the lantern while James and Doodle danced and pranced like boxers, playfully punching their fists at each other. On the night in 1937 when Joe Louis knocked out James Braddock in the eighth round, Vodie decided he had to have a radio of his own. Next day, he ordered a Philco from the Sears, Roebuck catalogue. Waiting for it to arrive in the mail created much excitement in a family that had so little. The children had no toys, games, or books, other than schoolbooks.

Once the radio arrived, Vodie placed it on the table near his rocking chair and ordered the boys not to touch it. He did not want the battery to run down. Every day as they ate dinner, they listened to the news and then to *Midday Merry-Go-Round*, a country music program, featuring such guests as Tennessee Ernie Ford, Roy Acuff, and Minnie Pearl. After dinner, Vodie always rested for a full hour, listening to the music show. He believed in letting the plow mules rest for an hour at midday, too. Then the radio stayed off until he returned for supper and to listen to the news and the commentators—H. V. Kaltenborn, Gabriel Heater, and Lowell Thomas. Sometimes, though, after his father left, Doodle would turn the radio on low and switch the station to some program he wanted to hear. He never quite succeeded in setting the dial back exactly where his dad had it set. His dad always knew that Doodle, not James, had fiddled with it and would bark, "Doodle, keep your hands off this radio!"

The only program that the entire family enjoyed was the *Grand Ole Opry*, and their favorite singers were Tennessee Ernie Ford and Ray Acuff, whose "Great Speckled Bird" gave Doodle goose bumps. The boys loved to hear Uncle Dave Macon pick the banjo, and they enjoyed the comic pair of Oswald and Rachel. Oswald had a raucous laugh which Doodle imitated—all too often to suit his family. Doodle and James learned songs from listening to the Opry, and they'd put on shows for the family and for anyone else who would listen. They'd sing and tap their feet as they strummed imaginary banjos and guitars.

In 1943 Vodie, with the help of his neighbor Jess Erington, finished building a new house for his family, right next to their old house. It took three years to build and fulfilled Lexie's longing for a place of her own. This new house had four large rooms, and each room had two large windows. Although it wasn't insulated, it had double walls and stayed warm during the winter. Vodie put a shingled roof on it instead of tin and hung screens on all the windows. He even made screen doors and covered the floors with linoleum. The house had no running water or electricity, but he bought a couple of the newfangled lamps called Aladdins, the next best thing to electric lights. Unlike the old kerosene lamps that lit up only a small area, the Aladdins, with their net-covered cones inside the dome, actually put light out over the entire room.

By the time this house was finished, Bill, the oldest child, had enlisted in the armed service; Herschel, Hobert, and Lillian had married and moved away. Only James and Doodle were still at home. They were inseparable companions and great friends.

The Floyds' place was three miles from Pilot Oak and hard to get to because it was so far back in the woods. There was no road to it—only a dirt lane, two and a quarter miles long. Neither cars nor milk and ice trucks could travel it. Hard rains would wash gullies so deep in it that it was hard even to walk down it, much less drive a wagon. Vodie always packed dirt back into these gullies when the earth dried out so that he could use the wagon. Despite the shape it was in, the lane was well traveled several times a day, every day, by Doodle and James as they went about their chores.

Until Vodie sold them, the cows were the brothers' biggest responsibility. First thing every morning, James and Doodle would go to the barn, feed the cows, and prepare to do the milking. As the cows were munching their corn, the boys would sit on stools while holding two-gallon milk buckets tightly between their legs. Sometimes their legs would get so tired they'd quiver uncontrollably. But the buckets had to be held tightly because the cows would kick them over any time they got a notion to do so.

Sitting on the windowsills nearby were four cats, waiting patiently for their breakfast. Now and then the boys would aim a cow's teat toward the cats and shoot a thin stream of milk to them. The cats could catch the milk every time.

After the morning milking was done, the boys would let the cows go out into the pasture to graze until late afternoon. Then they'd herd them into the milk barn, feed, and milk them again. After an evening of milking in the summer, the boys would put the cans filled with fresh milk into a large vat inside the milk shed. The vat was filled with cool water that had been hauled from their cistern. In the summer it was difficult to keep the milk from spoiling.

Before daybreak every morning, the first sound from the main road would be the clattering of the empty galvanized cans on the Pet Milk Company truck coming from Mayfield. The truck driver would collect the freshly filled milk cans and leave clean empties for the evening milking. He drove from farm to farm, if it were possible to do so. However, those few farmers who lived at the end of narrow lanes, as the Floyds did, had to haul their milk cans down the lane to the main road so the truck could pick them up there. Every morning James and Doodle had to haul the full milk cans in a large wheelbarrow (one with a steel wheel) down the lane to the main road, where the milk truck driver picked them up as soon as he could. The wheelbarrow was heavy and hard for young boys to roll. But they did the job. After unloading the cans, they ran the empty wheelbarrow back to the house and had breakfast. All that physical labor made them very strong.

By the time they had finished eating breakfast, the milk truck would have passed, collected the filled cans, and left the clean empties. So the boys would have to run back to the main road again to retrieve the empties. The rest of the morning they cut wood for the stove, mowed fields, cleaned weeds from the fences, spread clean sheets on the roof and laid sliced apples on it to dry, and worked in the garden with their mother. At noon every Monday, Wednesday, and Friday, the ice truck left the Floyds a hundred-pound block of ice on the main road for the boys to take home. Carrying that heavy block of ice wasn't an easy task. James would grab one end of the burlap sack and Doodle the other end, and off they'd go.

Even at age fourteen Doodle could be quite a charmer. (Photo courtesy of Charles Floyd)

They took turns being out in front because the lead man got the back of his legs and his ankles banged up by the ice.

Ice was a valuable commodity in those days. Some people stored it in little sheds built on the north side of their houses. Others had wooden ice boxes lined with tin in their kitchens or on their back porches. Doodle's father stored their ice in a box that he fixed into a hole in the back yard. Padded with sawdust for insulation and covered with old quilts, it was the only refrigeration they had until the late 1950s.

By early afternoon every day for years, Doodle and James had walked eight to twelve miles just doing their chores, excellent training for an athlete. They were getting stronger while increasing their endurance level.

In the afternoons James usually stayed at home with his mother while Doodle went to Pilot Oak to find Howie and then to see if the older boys would let them play a game of basketball with them. In the early 1940s Robert Wagoner, four or five years older than Doodle and Howie, smoothed the dirt court across the street in front of his dad's store in Pilot Oak. He cut and trimmed a small tree to make a goalpost and then nailed up a nice backboard with a real goal on it. After that he bought a brand-new basketball from the sporting goods store in Fulton. Howie and Doodle used to watch Robert and the others play and hungrily wait for an invitation to join them. After the older boys realized how good the younger two were, they welcomed them into their games.

Later, Howie and Doodle would have had a hard time getting to Cuba for games had it not been for Robert. A loyal friend, Robert on many nights drove them to Cuba and then back home again in his car. Coach Story never came after them and their parents never drove them to the school.

When Howie and Doodle weren't playing ball, they were running. Running especially appealed to them because it was free and easy. They could go as far and as fast for as long as they wanted. Howie was built for speed. His leg muscles were tapered and hard, as if they had been hand-built for a runner. He ran so fast he looked as though he were airborne. Gangling and awkward-looking, Doodle did not look like a runner, but he was a powerful one. Often in the long unhurried days of summer, the two boys would race to Cuba and back, a distance of sixteen miles or so. Their ability as runners later gave them an advantage on the hardwood where they played a fast game, running up and down the court sometimes keeping the ball from even touching the floor.

Although other children would start out playing tag with them, no matter who was tagged, Doodle would always end up alone chasing Howie, the fastest runner of them all. Many times their race would last all day until dark. With their heads held firm and straight, and their feet rising off the ground as if they were touching hot coals, they'd run for miles around Pilot Oak. When they got tired, they'd sit under a shade tree and rest—always maintaining between them whatever distance Howie had earned over Doodle. If Doodle began to sneak in closer, Howie would take off again.

They were often seen running up and down the main road in Pilot Oak pretending they had a basketball and tossing it between them. They were so in sync with each other that they could make all their fancy moves and work out all their routines with nothing more than their imagination. No other boys in the area played as earnestly as they did, nor were others even interested in playing with an imaginary basketball. The old folks enjoyed watching the two run, jump, fake dribble, shoot—all without a ball—but they often wondered "if them boys would ever amount to anything!"

CHAPTER 6

HOWIE CRITTENDEN

"GOD TEMPERS THE WIND TO THE SHORN LAMB."
—HENRI ESTIENNE

Pilot Oak, Kentucky—1933–1943. Howie and Helen, his twin sister, were the youngest of ten children born to Willie and Alta Ruth Crittenden on March 13, 1933. When the twins were born in Pilot Oak, Alta was forty-one years old—too old, the other women used to say, to have another baby, much less two at one time. The twins must have been a big surprise for Willie and Alta Ruth for they came along at a time when she thought her child-bearing days were over. Norman, their youngest, was nine years old when she became pregnant with the twins. Her pregnancy was an uncomfortable one: Her belly got as big as a barrel, and each baby weighed more than eight pounds. An old neighbor woman and Dr. Page delivered the twins in the Crittendens' home.

Although she was older than the mothers of Howie and Helen's friends, Alta Ruth looked even older than her age. She was tall and gaunt with limp brownish gray hair and soft brown eyes. Her complexion was dark and leathery from years of working outdoors. She had a way of tucking her head down toward her right shoulder as if she wanted only the left side of her face to show. A wine red birthmark that started in her hairline went down one side of her forehead and covered most of her right eye and her right cheek. Self-conscious about the mark, she tried to conceal it by wearing her long straight

Howie Crittenden, shown here in his senior
yearbook photo as Mr. Cuba High. (Cuba
school yearbook photo)

hair parted on the left side and pulled down slightly over the right side
of her face. She plaited her hair into one long braid, tied the end of
the braid with a piece of twine, and laid it over her right shoulder.

Willie Crittenden, Howie's dad, was crippled. Childhood
polio had left his legs twisted, with one about three inches shorter
than the other. Although he had a severe limp that caused painful
back problems, he worked without complaining. Willie Crittenden
had no knowledge of nor interest in athletics. For as long as everyone in Pilot Oak could remember, Willie complained about his
youngest son's wanting to play basketball all the time. The boy, he
grumbled, never wanted to help him in the tobacco field. It wasn't
until Howie's junior year in high school that Willie went to see his
son play ball. He went then only because everybody in Pilot Oak

41

had been talking so much about Howie's remarkable athletic ability that he needed to see for himself what they were talking about. Alta Ruth showed no more interest in her son's passion for basketball than Willie did. She never saw Howie play any of his high school games. But after he got to be a junior and had made quite a name for himself, she listened to the Mayfield radio station broadcasts of the games. Perhaps the Crittendens didn't attend games because they did not own a car and had no way to get to and from them. Whatever their reason, they never gave their boy encouragement to continue in sports.

For most of his life, Willie farmed, first by sharecropping and later by whittling out a living off his own land. It was only after the twins had graduated from high school and Howie had left for Murray State Teachers College that Willie got a steady paying job working on roads for the state highway department. It was a job given to him by some Graves County politicians after Howie had agreed to attend and play basketball for Murray State.

While his ten children were growing up, Willie farmed, although he was never successful at it. From the time the twins were born until World War II started, he worked as a sharecropper, moving his family several times from farm to farm in and around the Cuba-Pilot Oak area. He raised corn, sweet potatoes, and dark-fired tobacco.

Alta Ruth worked outside as hard as any man. Every year she planted a large garden and canned many jars of vegetables and fruits, enough to last her family until the next summer. When she was lucky enough to have a cow, she made butter and cheese. She also made most of her family's clothes and quilts by hand.

The flimsy three-room house the Crittendens lived in when the twins were infants was made out of logs that had not been weatherboarded over. It was drafty and cold. In the winter snow would blow in through the cracks; in the summer, rain and insects. The holes in the walls and floors got to be a serious problem because they were rat holes, something the Crittendens didn't know about until after they moved in. At that time all ten children were living with their parents in this three-room shanty. One night shortly after they moved in, a rat got on the bed with the two older boys—W. A. and Norman—and bit W. A. on the toe. That's how bold and bad the rats were. Just after that incident a chicken snake got into the house from a hole in the floor in the kitchen. After killing it with a broom, Alta Ruth sat on a stool in the kitchen and quietly cried over the hopelessness of her situation. That house was no different from many of the others that sharecroppers had to live in. Yet the people who lived in them had no alternative—indifferent landowners knew that and provided nothing better.

The Crittendens eventually moved into a larger house on the Effie Morris farm. It was a patched-up old dogtrot, a log house typical in style to those built in the Purchase in the 1850s. It had two large square rooms opening onto a central hall, which was called a dogtrot. This hall was used to wash and hang clothes and store firewood, tools, crocks, and buckets. The small kitchen in the rear had not originally been attached to the house, but someone at some time had attached it by tacking it with weatherboarding to the house. Each of the two rooms had a fireplace, one being used for cooking. This house was way off to itself in the back of a field with no neighbors nearby.

All day long in the summertime, the twins would play in the fields, gullies, and ditches around their house. With no other children to play with them, Howie and Helen became inseparable. Their only playmate was their solid white dog, part collie, whom they named Collie. She stayed with them everywhere they went and protected them from snakes. They'd had no toys except their Tom Walkers—stilts that their older brother Norman had made for them out of poles. When they tired of walking on those poles, they spent hours on summer afternoons making frog houses. They made these by putting their feet in the dirt and covering them with a lot of mud, which they patted down tightly and let dry while keeping their feet perfectly still. Having to remain still was good training in body control for Howie. They'd do only one foot at a time, of course, and good ones were hard to make. Once the mud was dry, they'd ease the foot out carefully so the house did not crumble. Then they'd decorate it with little leaves, wildflowers, and berries. For children like them, play required being inventive.

From the time he was small, Howie got into more accidents than his brothers and sisters did because he liked to compete. His dad called it showing off. One such accident occurred soon after his oldest brother, W. A., sent the twins a new red tricycle for their fifth birthday—the first present that they had ever received. They took turns riding it around the yard. Howie loved riding it fast down a hill where the yard sloped toward the dirt road. Trying to go faster than Helen had done, he rode that tricycle down that hill without putting his feet to the pedals. Going far too fast, he hit a rock, flipped over, and broke his left arm. When his mother saw it, she knew that the break was a bad one—one that she could not set. "We've got to git to Doc Page," she said as she grabbed a basket of eggs, ran to the barn, and hitched the mule to the wagon. While Howie cried and begged not to go, she and Helen sat silently the nine miles to Cuba. Having no cash, she gave Dr. Page the eggs for payment.

There was never any money in the Crittenden household, not even for necessities—like medical care. Two of the Crittenden children died as infants, perhaps from lack of medical attention as many children in other families did back then. Alta Ruth used folk remedies to treat her children. When Howie was six, he cut his foot badly on a piece of dirty broken glass. This was before tetanus shots and antibiotics were available. His mother applied the standard remedy of her time and place: She poured coal oil into the wound and wrapped his foot with clean rags until it healed.

Another time, while building a fire in the coal stove, Howie burned his hand so badly the skin slipped off. Believing that she had power to blow heat out of burns, his mother held his hand and blew into the burned area for several seconds. Then she mixed water with flour and baking soda and packed the paste all over the wound to draw the heat and soreness out. She repeated the process three or four times a day until the wound healed. Whenever the children had a fever, she'd brew a tea from feverfew, a wildflower with feathery leaves, that she gathered from fields and dried. For their stomachaches she made a tonic out of ginseng or a tea from chamomile leaves. For colds and pneumonia she soaked a rag in boiled asafetida and placed it on their chest. The fetid, ammonia-like odor from the "asafetidy," as they called it, was worse in some cases than the disease. Every spring she made cough syrup from violet blossoms, which she had gathered and soaked in water for a couple of days and then cooked with honey and lemon until the liquid thickened. She sealed the syrup into jars which she kept on the kitchen shelf. Whenever the children came down with the croup, she'd make them drink two big table-spoons of this syrup. She used "cloverine salve" for skinned places and bruises.

The summer before the twins were to enter the first grade, the Crittendens moved to Cuba, where Willie went to work as a janitor at the school. That fall, when Helen came down with the flu, Howie refused to go to school without her, and his parents didn't make him go. Then when *he* got sick, Helen didn't want to go without him. So both had to repeat the first grade, and that's why Doodle, the same age, was a grade ahead of them for a number of years.

In the first grade at the Cuba school, Howie got his taste of what it was like to receive recognition. When the teacher offered a prize to the student who colored a picture the neatest, Howie took the teacher's offer more seriously than the other children and won the contest. The teacher rewarded him with a piece of candy, two toy soldiers, and words of praise.

Willie did not like his janitorial job at school and returned to farming in Pilot Oak. While the twins were in the second grade at Pilot Oak school, Howie participated in the field day activities. This experience gave him his first understanding of what it means to compete. From the day he first heard about the field day races, he started training to win. Every afternoon he ran barefoot up and down the gravel road in front of his house, which was across the road from the school. He lost the race that year, but he won every year after that.

It was in the second grade, too, that he became interested in basketball. Pilot Oak had an exceptionally good basketball team that year. Twice a week the first, second, and third graders were permitted to watch the team practice in the school gym. Howie loved watching the players. When he went home in the afternoons, he'd try to imitate what he had seen the older boys do. A previous owner of the Crittendens' house had nailed a large tin molasses can on the side of the smokehouse and had left a rubber ball about the size of a tennis ball in the smokehouse. Only seven or eight years old then, Howie would spend hours alone tossing that ball through the tin can. Soon he was able to shoot the ball through the can from a little distance. When the ball split from age and use, he filled it with rags and kept playing. He played alone because, by this time, Helen was more interested in her schoolbooks and in helping her mother. It was not until he got acquainted with Doodle that Howie found someone who challenged him athletically.

The Crittendens went through many hard times, but the cruelest were from 1937 to 1942. The nation was in the throes of recession, and the Crittendens were among those designated by the government as "ill-housed, ill-fed, and ill-clad." By the spring of 1940, all of the Crittenden children except the twins had moved to Detroit and were working in factories. Willie was left with only seven-year-old Howie to help him finish getting his crop in. To get to his tobacco patch, he had to walk nearly a mile through a pasture that had several cows and a Jersey bull, which had horns and weighed nearly a thousand pounds. His coat had a beautiful dark sheen to it, meaning he was at least five years old. The older that bulls get, the meaner they are, and this bull had a bad reputation. He was devilish and moody; sometimes he'd be docile as a rabbit, and other times he'd be mean as the devil, going after horses, mules, and men with a ferocity that few could survive.

All that year Willie got across the field safely without the bull ever paying much attention to him. But the first morning that Howie accompanied his dad, things were different. Depressed about his brothers' leaving and about having to work in the tobacco field,

Howie burst into tears as he and Willie were crossing the field. The bull heard him and charged toward them. Terrified, father and son darted into a thorny thicket of blackberry bushes in front of a maple tree and then climbed the tree. That old bull stayed near the thicket, stomping bushes down, pawing the dirt, snorting, and bellowing for an hour before he finally got tired and wandered back into the pasture. When Willie and Howie finally reached the tobacco patch, their arms and faces were scratched and bloody. Howie pleaded with Willie not to make him go through that field again. But Willie answered, "Son, that old bull ain't the worst thing you gonna haf to deal with as you get older. Git your shoes and come on."

They planted corn, tobacco, sweet potatoes, and an acre of peanuts. Little did they realize that it would be the peanuts that would get them through that winter. Hard rains during the summer turned the fields into sloppy mud, and the tobacco and corn rotted. Only the sweet potatoes and the peanuts survived. Likewise, Alta's garden did poorly. After all the food that Alta had canned from the previous year's garden was used up, only the peanuts were left. She roasted them, parched them, fried them, fixed them every which way. The Crittendens ate peanuts every day all that winter long. Their charge account at Wagoner's was already more than they could ever pay, and they were embarrassed to ask Fred Wagoner for more credit. Without cows, corn, or chickens, they had nothing to trade.

Farmers had not shared in the nation's general prosperity during the 1920s. During the Great Depression of the 1930s, many big farms had been subdivided or sold so their owners could pay taxes. Although the economy improved during 1935 and 1936 as a result of President Franklin Delano Roosevelt's government spending, it bottomed out suddenly in the summer of 1937, and the nation went into a recession. Two million people were out of work. At Roosevelt's request, Congress allocated nearly four billion dollars for public works. Roosevelt's Farm Tenant Act passed by Congress in 1937 made loans available to help farmers, but for most it was too late.

Drastic changes in farming and raising livestock created problems for small farmers such as Willie Crittenden. Tractors, combines, and cultivators made it possible to work more acres, but they were expensive to buy and to operate. Farmers who bought the machinery had to sell their grain to buy gasoline to run it. Before, they had been able to feed their horses and mules with grain they raised at no cost. Many farmers, like Willie, accustomed to working with a mule and plow, could not adapt to the new methods and could not afford the fertilizer and the equipment—even if they learned to use them.

The Crittendens, along with many others during those dark days, looked for help from the government's Works Progress Administration (WPA), one of Roosevelt's New Deal programs. Large yellow government trucks came around regularly in the rural communities to distribute what were called "commodities"—foods with long shelf life such as flour, corn meal, cheese, dried beans and peas, baking powder, salt, baking soda, sugar, and canned foods. If it had not been for those commodities and the peanuts, the Crittendens would not have survived the winter. The trucks also distributed sweaters and coats. All the clothes looked alike, so everyone knew where your clothes came from.

When one of her little classmates visited Helen after school that winter, she was surprised to see that the only thing Mrs. Crittenden served for their supper was one small can of potted meat and some crackers. This poor nutrition as he was growing up affected Howie and his stamina to some degree and caused him to have serious problems with his teeth. But it also toughened him, teaching him to adjust to whatever deprivation befell him and to do his best in spite of the circumstances.

CHAPTER 7

DEE-TROIT CITY
BLUES

"IT IS HOPE WHICH MAINTAINS MOST OF MANKIND."
—SOPHOCLES

Michigan—1943–1945. Knowing that his family couldn't
go through another season like that one, Willie decided to go to
Detroit to find work. As soon as he had saved enough money, he
would then send for Alta and the twins. Before he left in late spring
1943, he moved them from Pilot Oak into the house his oldest
daughter, Emily, and her husband had just vacated by moving to
Detroit. Alta and the twins would live there until school was out,
and then they'd leave for Detroit.

This house was near the Kentucky-Tennessee border on Kentucky Highway 166, with one side of the road in Kentucky and the
other in Tennessee. Located in an isolated area, it was situated a little over a mile from a little place called Dukedom and three miles
south of Pilot Oak. The area was known for moonshining, killings,
fightings, and gambling, and it was not the ideal place for a woman
to live alone with two small children and no transportation. Now
that Willie was not sharecropping, they had no mule and wagon,
items the landowner had provided.

To the twins' delight, Emily had left her pet, an old bulldog
named Jiggs, behind for them and for their protection. Jiggs chased

49

away stragglers and drunks who occasionally wandered into the yard at night. He was also a companion for Collie, their beloved pet for many years. The other good thing about living in that house, aside from the fact it was rent free, was that their neighbors were the Floyds, whose farm was a mile across the field. It was here that Howie and Doodle got to be great friends, spending much of their time together in school and out of it.

After school each day, they'd go to one or the other's home, help with chores, and then play. Part of the time, they'd chase each other for hours, running barefoot all over the fields. Other times, they played basketball. Emily's husband had nailed an old basket on the side of the barn and had left his basketball for Howie to play with. Howie and Doodle played with that ball until it fell apart. Then they stuffed it with old rags, wrapped it with binder twine, and played some more.

This was the year they first got to see a high school varsity team play. Once or twice a week, their teacher would take all the boys in the class upstairs to the gymnasium to watch them. On a couple of occasions they got to watch an afternoon game. On some days, she'd turn the boys loose in the gym, giving them a rubber ball with which to play. It had no air in it, so they couldn't dribble it. All they could do was run up and down the court, trying to get the ball away from whoever had it and then throwing it at the basket. Howie and Doodle managed to keep the ball to themselves while the other boys chased after them.

Willie got a job as janitor at Michigan Tool Company in Detroit, and by early April he had sent Alta Ruth an envelope stuffed with three bus tickets, two twenty-dollar bills, and a note saying he had rented one of those "gov'mint apartments" and wanted her and the twins to come to Detroit. Not one to express emotions, he simply wrote, "I miss you. I wont you all here soon."

Just as they were preparing to go, Howie came down with scarlet fever. In those days scarlet fever, like polio and lockjaw, was a dreaded disease. Once it was determined that a person had it, a quarantine sign had to be posted on the house where the infected person

50

lived. No one inside the house was supposed to come out, and no one from the outside could go in. A loyal friend, Lexie Floyd, brought Alta Ruth sacks of groceries from the commodity truck and set them on the steps of the house. She waved to Alta and the twins as they smiled to her from the window. Fortunately, neither Helen nor Alta came down with scarlet fever. After Howie recovered completely, Alta made arrangements for them to leave for Detroit.

Before daybreak one morning that summer of 1943, Lexie, James, and Doodle arrived in their horse-drawn wagon to take the Crittendens to the bus station in Fulton, Kentucky. For the twins, the saddest thing about their departure was discovering that they had to leave Collie and Jiggs behind. While grief-stricken Howie stared at his mother in disbelief, Helen pursed her lips and stubbornly refused to get into the wagon without her pets. Angrily, Alta Ruth snatched the child up and plopped her down on the back seat of the wagon as the dogs quizzically watched their owners prepare to leave. For the full nine miles to the bus station, Helen sobbed fitfully, while Howie lay silently on his back staring at the faded purple sky. For years after, whenever he closed his eyes, he could see Collie and Jiggs as they appeared that morning, their images indelibly stamped on the back of his eyelids.

This trip—the Crittendens' first out of the Jackson Purchase—was frightening. When they arrived at the noisy crowded bus station in Detroit, Willie was nowhere to be seen. With Helen clinging to her, Alta Ruth sat tensely on a bench holding in her lap the feed sacks stuffed with their possessions and clenching the money Willie had sent her. Howie stood nearby scanning the crowd for his dad. When Howie finally spotted him limping through the entrance, he yelled, "There's Poppa!" and ran toward him. Willie held the boy tightly in his arms for a long minute, and then the two of them went over to where Alta Ruth and Helen were standing. As Willie wrapped one arm around Alta and drew her closely to him, he scooped Helen up in his other arm and hugged and kissed them both. Then he said cheerfully, "I've a taxi waiting. Let's hurry!"

The cab drive to their apartment was a jerky one, stopping and starting along the crowded narrow streets, full of cars and trucks, noisy sirens, smoke, and dust. Sidewalks were filled with zoot suiters, guys who wore blousy-legged pants that fitted tightly round the ankles, big boxy jackets, wide hats with flat brims, and long gold watch chains. They roamed the streets all hours and gang fights broke out routinely. Whizzing by rows and rows of narrow ugly little houses that bordered the streets, the cab finally pulled up in front of a two-storied framed apartment house that looked exactly like the other four ugly ones across the street.

The Crittendens' new home was a four-room upstairs apartment, sparsely furnished, with no yard for the children to play in. The twins were now confined to this cramped apartment because Alta Ruth was afraid to let them go outside. Living in Detroit required an adjustment that none of them could make. They had grown too accustomed to the freedom that farm life provided, and they were depressed even though they were reunited with Emily and her husband. For weeks the twins came home from school crying every afternoon. The large school, the strict teachers, the crowded classrooms, the traffic, the sirens for simulated air raids that sent the students crawling under their desks—all were too much for the twins at first. Most damaging of all was their inability to keep up academically.

One day after the teacher talked about the importance of good posture and announced that she would give a reward to the student who sat the straightest all day, Howie saw the offer as an opportunity to succeed in at least one thing. That entire day, he sat, stood, and walked ramrod straight. He won the award along with the teacher's praise, and her praise gave him more confidence than she realized. If ever a child yearned for approval, it was Howie. Soon he and Helen began to excel in reading and math, and both improved their grammar and speech.

After a year in Detroit, the Crittendens moved into another apartment in a slightly better neighborhood. It was here that Alta Ruth received a telegram one winter afternoon in 1944 saying that

W. A., her oldest son, a corporal in the army, was missing in action. A few weeks later, when she received another telegram saying W. A. had been taken prisoner by the Germans, she collapsed on the couch and sobbed for hours. She felt that the world she knew was falling apart. Although she wasn't told at the time, W. A. had been captured near Dijon, France, while serving in Gen. George S. Patton's hard-driving U.S. Third Army. He barely survived that terrible winter in the prisoner-of-war camp.

The twins that year transferred to Trumley Elementary School, where physical education classes were required and where Howie had a chance to play basketball. When the other children and the instructor saw him shoot the ball with a two-handed set shot, their eyes widened. "Hey, where did you learn to shoot like that?" the teacher asked. Later she told him, "You've got a natural knack for handling that ball. And you move like lightning. You could be a great basketball player some day." Then when she had the class shoot layups, Howie again did better than any of the others and that made him feel really good.

The twins went on to do well in school. Helen was chosen to work on the yearbook, and Howie was selected to be one of the "safety guards," a position that made him feel proud because only students who had earned the teachers' trust were selected. By this time Howie had a paper route and a secondhand bicycle, one with no fenders. Although he had to get up at four every morning to make his deliveries before school, he didn't care. He gave the money he earned to his mother to save for their return home to Kentucky.

Shortly before the war ended, a letter arrived saying that W. A. was among those soldiers released from a German prison camp and would be discharged with honors. He and his younger brother Norman, who also was in the army, would be back in the States soon and they'd all be home, together again, in Kentucky.

After school closed that summer of 1945, the Crittendens returned to Pilot Oak. The four-room house they moved into was next door to Wagoner's store, and it had a switchboard in the front room, put there the previous year when some Pilot Oak men created a battery-operated, party-line telephone system for the community. Instead of paying rent, the Crittendens agreed to operate the switchboard. The job fell to Alta, and it was a confining one. No call could be made without going through that switchboard, and the lines ran all the way to Dukedom and to Fulton, Tennessee.

With the money he had saved by working in Detroit, Willie bought a thirty-acre farm, a mule, a mare, four cows, fifty chickens, three pigs, a plow, a wagon, and some farm tools. This farm was about two miles from where the Crittendens had earlier lived in Pilot Oak, and it adjoined the Floyds' place.

Being home again and having Doodle to run and play basketball with made Howie happy. But his return meant much more to Doodle, for it helped fill a void that had tragically occurred the previous year.

CHAPTER 8

DEATH STARTLES AND STINGS

"BY GRIEF THE SOUL IS TORN ASUNDER."
—PROVERBS 27:14

Pilot Oak, Kentucky—August 5, 1944. The most important person in Doodle's young life was his older brother James. Doodle adored James, and James loved his little brother with all his heart. They worked and played together. As it always does with best friends, some bickering went on between them occasionally but it always ended in laughter. Until James turned thirteen and Doodle ten in 1944, they were constant companions. But as soon as James reached his teenage years, he wanted to have some time of his own to read or to just be alone. He had outgrown most of the games that his younger brother still enjoyed playing. Loving him as he did, Doodle was puzzled by what he thought was rejection. Then, too, their mother had extracted a solemn promise from him that he would always stay with James to see to it that he did not hurt himself when he had a seizure, for James had epilepsy.

Tall, muscular, and handsome, James weighed 175 pounds by the time he was thirteen. He had thick blond straight hair that he parted on the side and kept neatly cut and combed. He had a smooth olive complexion, denim-blue eyes, a square jawline, and resolute expression. He looked like the archetypal American youth—a poster boy. Not only was he handsome, but he was good-natured, intelligent, and kind. All through school he made straight A's and he also saw to it that Doodle did well in his schoolwork. James, unlike Doodle, was an avid reader, and he won awards nearly every year for reading more library books than anyone else at the school. James read big books, too, books that the other kids called real hard; he didn't just read the Zane Grey and Tarzan series. He was elected president of his class and also the president of the Future Farmers of America, an organization that the school required all boys to join. James was much loved not only by his family, but by his friends, teachers, and folks in Pilot Oak. Everyone who knew the Floyds knew that the family was immensely proud of James and had great expectations for him. They knew, too, that his father lived vicariously through the boy, for James was all that Vodie was not and yet wished to be.

The Floyds did not favor James over Doodle; it was just that Doodle pestered them often because he was mischievous. He loved to play and run and make people laugh. He would do just about anything to get a laugh and avoid work. None of the other four children in the family were quite like him. His mother would often shake her head in dismay, saying as much as she hated to admit it, she believed that Doodle got his stubbornness and fondness for mischief from her side of the family—from some of those "awful Jacksons from Tennessee." Her deepest fear was that her youngest child would turn out to be like her own father, John Jackson, a bootlegger and braggart who married seven times. On the other hand, James was more like Tom Floyd, the brother of Vodie's father. An honest, hardworking man, Tom was admired and respected by all who knew him.

Around the age of six or seven, James fell from a moving wagon and was knocked unconscious. After he awakened, he seemed perfectly all right. Were it not for a bad bruise on the side of James's head, no one would have known that he had even been injured. He continued to grow and develop as any other normal child. But when he got to be around eleven, he began having seizures. His first attack occurred one morning shortly after Christmas while his dad was working in Detroit. His mother was frightened, not knowing what to think. The old folks in Pilot Oak said that children (like James) would sometimes outgrow such "fits" and that nothing could be done but pray that James would outgrow them. Since the child was otherwise healthy, strong, and intelligent, she did not take him to Dr. Page.

What worried Lexie more than anything was the possibility that he might injure himself in a fall during one of the attacks. During the seizures, he lost consciousness, fell to the floor, shaking and jerking, perspiring profusely, sometimes biting the inside of his mouth and tongue badly. The seizures lasted only a few seconds, stopping as quickly as they started, yet leaving him quite drowsy. Sometimes he'd sleep for a couple of hours after having an attack. Fearing that he would hit his head or choke or cut his tongue, Lexie explained to Doodle how to take care of James and said never—never—never leave James alone. "Pretend," she said, "that you are the older, stronger one. You look after James."

The seizures were unpredictable, coming quickly without warning. James would go for weeks without having one and then have ten to fifteen in one day. Coping with epilepsy was difficult for the child. It limited his freedom to do things he wanted to do. He couldn't ride a bike because riding it could have been too dangerous for him if he were in the wrong place at the wrong time. He couldn't participate in some school or church activities because he feared he might disrupt them. He couldn't go fishing alone or for walks. Someone always had to be near him. Having spells at school in front of the others was painfully embarrassing. Whenever James had an attack at school, the principal would call Doodle out of his class to come stay with James until he recovered. Not many people in Pilot Oak ever saw James without Doodle nearby.

When the brothers got off the school bus every afternoon at Wagoner's, they walked the three miles home. They were always careful while crossing the little wooden bridge down from Martha Casey's house because one time earlier, James had had a seizure on

James Floyd looked like the archetypal American
youth—a poster boy. Not only was he handsome,
but he was good-natured, intelligent, and kind.
(Photo courtesy of Charles Floyd)

the bridge. He fell down and started jerking and rolling. Terrified
that James would drown if he rolled into the creek below, Doodle,
who was only a third grader at the time, jumped on top of his
brother's twisting body and lay holding him in place as best he
could. It was a frightening experience that James did not remember, but one that Doodle never forgot.

During the winter that James had his first seizures, no one
wrote to tell Vodie, who was working in Detroit, about them.
When he returned in the spring and saw his son having a seizure,
he was shocked and frightened. He immediately took the child to
Cuba to Dr. Page, who suggested that they go to a specialist in

Mayfield the next day. The Mayfield physician prescribed a new drug—Dilantin. It had been developed in 1938 and was working miracles for people with epilepsy. It was expensive and required regular monitoring by Dr. Page, and James had to take it daily. "You cannot miss a dose! Unless I tell you to stop taking it, do not stop," the Mayfield physician instructed the boy and his father.

Once the dosage of Dilantin was adjusted for James's body, the seizures stopped. Dilantin gave the boy the confidence and the freedom to do some things that he had never done without great fear—like stand up before a group, perform in a play, talk, or read in class. He had a lovely tenor voice and could sing baritone, too, but he had never joined the chorus. Dilantin permitted him to enjoy performing.

In the summer of 1944, their dad bought James and Doodle a pair of secondhand lawn mowers and got them a job mowing the two cemeteries in Pilot Oak. They made good money that they saved in a used Bull Durham tobacco sack and hid under the root of the huge chinaberry tree in their backyard. At the base of this ancient tree, several large roots had humped up out of the ground, providing ideal spaces, secret and dry, for the boys to hide their chewing tobacco and money.

August 5, 1944, was a blistering hot, humid day. After dinner, James and Doodle walked with their parents to Wagoner's where the folks had gathered to talk about war news and about whether Roosevelt, frail with ill health, ought to run for a fourth term. For most of that afternoon, as James, Doodle, and other boys played basketball in front of the store, the Floyds sipped icy cold Orange Crushes and talked quietly with their friends about the war, and about their sons in the service. Bill, the Floyds' oldest son, was in the army serving in the Pacific, and they worried about him all the time, especially after hearing that U.S. troops had landed on Guam on July 21. Everyone was tense after learning that young Clyde Pickens, the husband of one of Lexie's cousins, had been killed in action and that the Crittendens' oldest boy, W. A., had been captured by the Germans.

Around four o'clock that afternoon, Vodie told Lexie, "Let's get the boys and go home and fix some supper." James and Doodle took off running ahead of their parents and arrived at home long before them. Doodle often had headaches and that afternoon after playing basketball in the hot sun, he was suffering from a terrific headache that running home had made worse. Once he stepped into his front yard, instead of going into the house or around to the backyard as he usually did, he dropped to the ground and stretched out on his belly in the front yard under the big shade tree. With his head resting on his hands and turned toward the house, he watched James go around to the backyard. The house was built high off the ground and did not have any shrubbery around it, so Doodle could see plainly the yard behind the house. He watched James's legs going toward the outhouse, and then he closed his eyes and tried to nap. A few seconds later, he opened them again and watched for James to come out. Maybe twenty or so minutes passed before his parents got home and walked past him, still lying on his stomach on the ground. They went straight into the house without saying anything to him. Then Doodle saw his dad looking out the window at him. Next, he heard the back door open and slam shut. Through narrow slits of his eyes, he watched his father's legs go from the house toward the outhouse.

Suddenly, he heard a queer cry; it sounded like the cry of an injured animal. He jumped up when he realized it was his father, crying as if his soul was being torn from his body. Then he heard him shout, "Doodle! Run! Go get Dr. Page! Hurry, boy! Run! Run!" Knowing what must have happened, Doodle was filled with terror as he broke out running across the pasture two miles to their nearest neighbor's house. Breathless, with tears staining his face and his heartbeat pounding in his ears, he tried to explain to the elderly neighbor, Ed Rhodes, whom he woke from a nap, that James needed help. He cried, "Please, Mr. Rhodes, please. Poppa needs you to get Dr. Page! James has hurt himself bad!" Without asking any questions, the man quickly grabbed his hat, pulled up his suspenders, and jumped into his Model A. He spun out of his driveway, kicking up a mess of dust that settled on the boy's sweaty face. Doodle ran back to his house where he found his father cradling James in his arms, rocking back and forth, crying helplessly. His mother was kneeling near him. She was sobbing into her apron which she had pulled up around her face and was holding with the palms of both hands.

James was dead. He had had a seizure in the outhouse and had fallen, striking his head against the door. Dr. Page said an artery in James's neck had ruptured and that nothing could be done. The child had drowned in his own blood.

Later it was learned that James had stopped taking his Dilantin. A person in Pilot Oak, for some unknown reason, had told the boy he didn't need that expensive medicine and ought to quit taking it and stop wasting his folks' money. This person recommended some kind of tea made from ground-up wild plant leaves, saying that it would do just as well as anything store-bought. Whatever made the boy follow that person's deadly advice will never be known. But, apparently, he did follow it.

Just hours before his death, James had told his mother where he and Doodle had been hiding their savings. With eerie prescience, he also told her that if anything ever happened to him, he wanted her to get his sack which had almost seventeen dollars in it and buy herself a ring. He had often heard her admire the pretty gold rings she saw in the Sears, Roebuck catalogue. She never had a wedding ring, at least not a real one, and had always wanted a wide gold band. The morning that James told her about the money and ring, she didn't pay much attention to him. But after his death, she realized that he must have known what was to happen.

James was laid to rest in the old Pinson Graveyard, near Pea Ridge, where all the Jacksons are buried. He lies alongside his grandfather John Jackson and near his great-grandfather Clint Jackson and his brother Harold.

The death had a profound effect on the family. Vodie became even more of a loner—moody and melancholy. A tragic figure, he submerged himself in work, staying in the field far into the night.

61

The deeply saddened Floyd family gathered at the graveyard after James was buried. Pictured left to right are Doodle's dad, Vodie; mother, Lexie; older brothers, Hobert and Herschel; and sister, Lillian. Doodle is in front. (Photo courtesy of Charles Floyd)

When he did come in for meals, he ate silently and then sat in his rocking chair with his eyes closed, never talking to anyone unless he had to. He made it clear that he did not want to be talked to. For over a year, he never turned the radio on. With Lillian and all the boys except Doodle gone, the house was quiet. Lexie went about her duties listlessly. No longer did she hum or sing softly to herself while she worked.

Doodle, only eleven years old, was left alone much of the time to fend for himself. Not much attention was paid to his coming or going. Yet his sorrow may have been the most profound of all, for he could not escape thinking that had he followed James that day to the backyard, he could have saved him. His parents never said anything to him about that nor indicated that they thought he could have saved his brother. No one in Pilot Oak either said or appeared to think it. It was just that he thought it. "James would be alive," he often said to himself, "if I had followed him, if only I had been there to help him." His grief ran deep.

CHAPTER 9

ON THE IMPORTANCE OF ACTING RIGHT

"A WISE MAN MAKES HIS FATHER GLAD, BUT A FOOLISH SON IS A GRIEF TO HIS MOTHER."

—PROVERBS 10:1

Pilot Oak—1946–1947. Around the age of thirteen, Howie and Doodle got to thinking that they were grown-up. Doodle, especially, started thinking of himself as a big guy—chewing and spitting tobacco, comparing the budding bodices of female peers, and expanding his colorful vocabulary—all of which got him into varying degrees of trouble with his parents. One afternoon when his mother overheard him cussing, she washed his mouth out with a piece of soap and asked him, "Now, Charles, how tasty are your words?"

In those days it was nearly impossible for kids to get away with any kind of mischief because the folks in Pilot Oak, like the ones in Cuba, looked after each others' children. Some mothers worked in Mayfield at the Merit Clothing Company and did not get home in the evenings until 5:30 or 6:00, about the same time their husbands came in from the fields, and much later than their children returned home from school. Others, like Lexie Floyd, lived far out in the country and could not possibly know what their children were doing all the time. But parents did not worry, because every adult had authority to correct any child's behavior. Although the children were free to wander about, they were being seen by someone from a kitchen window, or back porch swing, or garden.

More than once Howie and Doodle experienced painful consequences as a result of Pilot Oak's collective effort to teach its children "to act right."

One sultry July afternoon, after they had finished their basketball game in front of the store while the "store setters" on the porch watched and egged them on, they longed for an ice-cold RC, a Tootsie Roll, or a Baby Ruth. But they didn't have a nickel between them. As they watched Mr. Wagoner ignore his customers and listened to his slurred speech, they realized that he had been sipping too much out of the old stained coffee cup that he kept filled with moonshine whiskey. After some whispering, they dashed back to Howie's house, next door to the store, and peeped in through the window to see if his mother was still sitting at her quilting rack piecing a quilt. Furtively, they ran around to the back of the house and swiped one of her chickens from the hen yard, poked the squirming thing into a croaker sack, and tied the sack. Doodle, the stronger of the two, tucked it tightly under his arm as they hurried off to the store where they nervously traded it for two RCs, two big Baby Ruths, two Tootsie Rolls, and two Tarzan comic books. Mr. Wagoner took the chicken out of the sack and tossed it into the pen he kept behind the store. In those days, with no refrigeration, chickens were not killed until they were ready to be cooked, and all the storekeepers had chicken coops behind their stores.

Mr. Wagoner's eyes had such a glassy vacant stare that afternoon that Doodle told Howie, "I don't think he'll even remember us being here today." After they had consumed their delightful treats, they figured they'd better get that chicken back to Howie's yard before his mother missed it. They stealthily slipped back behind the store and stole the same chicken, but instead of returning it to the hen yard, they decided to trade the chicken again for some more good stuff. And they did.

They had a great time, lying in the shade of the plum tree behind the store, planning future trades with Mr. Wagoner, all the while unaware that they had been under surveillance. By the time the boys got home, the informer had made her report. That night Howie and Doodle got a whipping they never forgot and a scalding lecture on stealing. For atonement, they had to apologize to the storekeeper and, for the remainder of the summer, they had to sweep out his store daily and keep the saplings away from his fence row. Their fathers asked the store setters to make sure that the boys fulfilled their obligations.

Each store had its own set of store setters, old men who sat at the store all day long. In Pilot Oak, a dozen or so old men, who called themselves the Great Fraternity of Mystic Knights of the Sea, gathered at Wagoner's every day and stayed until the store closed in the evening around nine. All were pipe smokers, their teeth worn down from years of clenching a pipe stem. In the winter the old men would sit on nail kegs around a Warm Morning stove, talk, play checkers, and visit with the folks that came in. They'd heat their coffee and roast sweet potatoes on top of the stove. In the summer they'd drink pop and sit on benches on the shady front porch. Members of this group included Fred Wagoner, Jack Olive, Red McClure, Vestal and Marvin Colthrap, Daris Emerson, Frank Morris, John Yates, and B. C. Lowery. Later, Howie and Doodle were inducted into this fraternity. Honorary members were Happy Chandler, governor of Kentucky, and Alben Barkley, vice president of the United States.

Inside the store in the winter and outside in the summer, they played checkers on a board they had made and painted themselves. They used Coke bottle caps for checkers; turned-up caps were reds, turned-down, blacks. They used to like to play checkers with Howie because he challenged them and with Doodle because of all the laughter he created by trying to cheat them. They also liked to take the two boys on some of their coon hunts.

The head of the coon hunters was Goble McClure, a big farmer who owned a hundred acres between Pilot Oak and Water Valley. He and his old hunting dog, a blue tic called Ole Blue, would come to the store in Goble's old pickup in the evenings.

Men in the community often gathered in local stores for hours of storytelling and checkers, although a favorite topic of discussion in the early 1950s was the exploits of the Cuba Cubs. Here, Coach Jack Story commands an attentive audience as he joins in to discuss basketball strategy. (*Paducah Sun Democrat* photo provided by Carolyn Story)

Ole Blue would ride in the front seat just like any other passenger. Friday nights were coon-hunting nights. If Doodle and Howie were around the store, they'd go along, too. Deep in the woods, the hunters would build a big campfire and sit around telling horror stories, such as the one they told the boys about the time panthers frightened their dogs so bad that the dogs wouldn't go back into the woods. Those stories were so frightening that Doodle would not walk home alone. He either stayed at Howie's house or Howie stayed at his. Whenever the two of them walked down that long dark lane to the Floyds', they'd walk cautiously, on the lookout for panthers and other savage beasts. Howie would look one way and Doodle the other.

The old men's favorite pastime was teasing kids and grown-ups alike. For instance, they made people get permits before doing such things as killing hogs, roofing a barn, or getting engaged to be married. If a man was seen doing woman's work, such as picking beans from a garden, he was fined. If found guilty, the defendant had to buy a cold drink for all the members who were at the store at the time the hearings were held. Howie's dad was their champion checkers player, and whenever an outsider, say from Lynnville or Dukedom, beat Willie at checkers, the Knights would fine the outsider. A few people in Pilot Oak unintentionally lent themselves to teasing more than others, but none more than Eddie Harper, the one-legged brother of Jack Harper who ran the store in Cuba.

For a long time Eddie Harper was the only person in Pilot Oak who owned an automobile. Pilot Oak, like Cuba back then, had no stoplights, but it had a stop sign at the intersection of Highway 94 and State Road 129. Eddie always sailed right across the intersection without ever stopping at the stop sign or even slowing down. Whenever he approached the intersection, he just blew his horn and went straight through. The store setters predicted that "Eddie would git his comeuppance."

One day while Howie and Doodle were running toward the store, they saw Eddie driving south down the middle of State Road 129. As Eddie approached the stop sign, he started blowing his horn but never slowed down. Suddenly, about the same time Eddie was heading south toward the intersection, Elbert Webb, home from Detroit to visit his parents in Pilot Oak, appeared out of nowhere on Highway 94, driving his brand-new Chevy. Doodle yelled, "We gonna see some excitement now!" Knowing that he had the right-of-way, Elbert was unaware of Eddie's custom of ignoring the rules of the road. Although you could hear Elbert's brakes screeching for a mile around, he couldn't stop in time to keep from crashing into Eddie's car, knocking it into the ditch. Neither man was hurt, but both cars were badly dented. Shocked and furious, Eddie got out yelling, waving his arms around, "Damnit, Elbert, didn't you hear me blow my horn?"

The Purchase is dotted with tiny little places like Pilot Oak, and each place has its colorful lore and colorful personalities. In Little Cubie, old Will Routen was the source of many tall tales. Routen, nicknamed "Old Boy," was a miser. The joke in Cuba was that he once dropped a dime in the haystack and his mule ate the hay. When Will realized what had happened to his dime, he grabbed ahold of that old mule's tail and followed the mule around in the field all day until he got his dime back. He lived in one of the poorest houses and rode the poorest-looking mule in the county. When his shoes burst apart from the soles, he continued to wear them after he clamped the toe to the sole with a hog's ring. He never wore socks no matter how cold it got and had no notion of health or hygiene. Dr. Page could never figure out how Will managed to live so long and told him, "You don't have a damn bit more business being out of the ground than a mole does!"

When he started his practice in Cuba in 1908, Dr. Page made his house calls on horseback over roads he described as "simply awful," then in a horse-drawn buggy or wagon, and finally, in 1916, in his first automobile, a Model T Ford. He drove it for years and then another much like it until the late 1940s, when he got a used World War II army jeep. Whatever he drove, he always liked to sing as he went along. The children used to listen for him coming down the road singing loudly: "Whoa! Mule, I tell you—Whoa! Mule I say! Keep holdin' on E-liza Jane! And don't fall off this stray!" Somehow just hearing him as he approached their house made patients feel better in most instances. When he started his practice, he said he "didn't have much medicine other than quinine for chills and calomel for worms." His success in healing often had as much to do with his personality as it did with medicine. In his case, the old notion that "the doctor is the medicine" was a fact. Believing that the course of many illnesses is influenced by the patient's frame of mind, Doc Page paid attention to his patients' fears and worries.

His sense of humor and his hearty laugh were disarming. Folks still laugh when they start to tell you about old Doc Page.

By the time he retired in the 1950s, Dr. Page had delivered nearly two thousand babies, including all the Cubs except Doodle. He was seldom paid in cash for any of his services, a fact that he only lamented in his diary. He and his wife, Era, and their four children—Ted, George, Hattie, and Beth—lived in a two-storied, white frame house, less than a quarter of a mile from the Cuba school. His office, a three-room white frame building next to his house, had a waiting room, an examining room, and an office combined with his pharmacy. On top of his medical supply cabinet, he kept a neat little stack of white envelopes. Joe Buddy, Donald, Howie, Jimmie Webb, Doodle, and others remember well how he used to pick up one of those little envelopes and blow into it to open it; then he'd reach for a bottle of pills, shake out a few of them into the envelope, seal it, and scribble in pencil some instructions on the front. Next he'd slap the envelope into the patient's hand and say, "Here, take these. They'll either cure you or kill you."

Always interested in education, Dr. Page was optimistic about the consolidation of schools in the Purchase, believing the central schools would be stronger. In 1946, when the high school at Pilot Oak was one of those closed and consolidated into the one at Cuba, the Cuba school had twelve grades, six teachers, and a principal who also coached and taught civics and physical education. Depending on farming conditions, perhaps 130 students attended grades eight through twelve and about 250, the elementary grades.

Neither Doodle nor Howie was happy about having to transfer to the Cuba school. A grade ahead of Howie, Doodle was the first to leave, and he did not make the transition easily or successfully.

During his first couple of weeks in the seventh grade, he ignored his mother's advice about "behaving, studying, and paying attention to the teachers." Although he'd leave for school and return home on the school bus each day, he would not stay at school all day. He'd eat his lunch and then leave to run around with older boys.

One afternoon while he was playing basketball with three dropouts in front of Harper's, he suddenly stopped in his tracks, listening intently. He thought he heard his dad's old Model A off in the distance. Back then, there were so few automobiles in the southern end of the county that anyone with a keen ear, like Doodle, could recognize the distinctive sound of each car. His head cocked to one side, Doodle stood looking down the road, shading his eyes with his hand, squinting hard to see as far as he could. "Nah, Poppa's in the field working at this time of day. T'ain't him," he assured himself. As he stood there looking down the road, he suddenly saw coming out of a cloud of dust, an old Ford sputtering along the road, barreling toward Cuba at its top speed—twenty-five miles an hour. Doodle stiffened with dread.

It seems that Joe McPherson, the young history teacher, unlike the lenient Pilot Oak teachers, had reported Doodle's numerous absences. Vodie did not take the news lightly. A no-nonsense, hard-working man, Vodie could not tolerate "idleness" or "foolishness" in any of his children and, much to his dismay, his youngest child seemed much too inclined to both.

When he saw his son standing in front of the store holding a basketball at one o'clock in the afternoon, when he should be in a classroom, Vodie became furious. He pulled his old car up to an abrupt stop, leaned over to the passenger side, and with his huge hand popped open the door, yelling to Doodle to "get in this car!" Then he gunned the motor and wrenched the wheel hard in the opposite direction, sped around a curve, swung into the school yard, and came to a screeching halt. Teachers and students ran to the windows. Right there, in front of the school with children and teachers watching, Vodie jumped out of the car and dragged Doodle out with him. He pulled a leather belt from his overalls pocket and gave his son three sound whops on the rear end with it. It was a humiliating experience for Doodle, who went on to fail the seventh grade anyway. He said he failed purposefully, so that he and Howie could be in the eighth grade together.

The one person who saved Doodle that year from quitting school, running away from home, and doing heaven knows what else, was Kindred Winston, the coach at the Cuba school. Mr. Winston knew that James's death had been hard on the child and on his family, and he figured that the boy needed attention that he was not getting from his grief-stricken parents. He thought that Doodle was capable of becoming a good student and a good athlete, for he had a remarkable natural ability for basketball. Mr. Winston made a point of speaking to Doodle every time he saw him and gave him a bit of encouragement on each occasion. He knew that keeping a troubled youngster, such as Doodle, involved in sports was the only way to keep him in school. After watching the boy on the basketball court, he would always say something like, "Say, I sure like your steady control of the ball," or "By next year, you'll make a great center and a rebounder on the team. The way you keep moving while holding your arms wide open and elbows up is great! Man, you've got the touch!" One day he told Doodle, "Say, you keep on doing what you're doing, and you'll be a great basketball star someday."

Eager to please Mr. Winston, Doodle did his schoolwork more attentively and seldom skipped class. At the end of the school year in 1947, however, when he learned that Mr. Winston was leaving Cuba to become principal of a high school in South Fulton, Tennessee, he became bitterly disappointed. He felt as if he were at loose ends again. Without a coach, Cuba would be without a basketball team.

CHAPTER 10

THE GREATEST SHOW ON EARTH—OR IN KENTUCKY

"IF YOU THINK LOSING WITH GOOD SPORTSMANSHIP IS AS GOOD AS WINNING,
THEN WHY IN HELL DO THEY KEEP THE SCORE?"
—ADOLPH RUPP

Kentucky—1945–1952. Small rural schools in Kentucky during the 1940s and early 1950s did not have football or baseball teams, because there weren't enough boys enrolled to fill out a football or baseball team roster. Nearly all children had farm duties, and their attendance at school depended on the season, the weather, and the crops. It was not uncommon for youths to drop out of school after they reached the seventh or eighth grades. Even if there had been enough players, the little schools could not afford to buy uniforms, pads, helmets, and cleats.

On the other hand, just about every little rural school had a basketball team and could afford a basketball and some kind of goalpost, if not uniforms, warm-ups, and basketball shoes. Players were considered lucky if they had jerseys, trunks, and shoes. Some teams played in overalls and work shoes. Regardless of how small they were, these schools took great pride in being successful at basketball. The competition was keen. About the only way for a boy

to get recognition as being someone other than a farmer was by playing basketball. The better the boys got at the sport, the more the
community rallied around them and vice versa: Each fed off the other.
In rural communities, basketball games were the chief source of entertainment then. In Graves County the gyms weren't large enough
to hold all those who wanted to see Cuba's games.

Recent school mergers and consolidations have produced a
smaller number of larger schools comprising basketball districts, but
in those days the tiny schools—like Cuba—flourished in terms of
community support while relishing the David-Goliath opportunities
now almost obsolete. A regular schedule of games in the forties and
fifties included the teams in each county. Graves County included
Cuba, Mayfield, Symsonia, Farmington, Sedalia, Wingo, Fancy Farm,
Lowes, and Melber. The coaches and principals—often they were the
same person—collaborated to set up the regular schedule for the season. Coaches were allowed to add to the schedule any out-of-region
or out-of-state games. Jack Story and a few others figured it was good
practice if their teams could play ones that were considered better
than theirs. Such competition gave the local boys broader experience
and an opportunity to test their skills against different defenses and
methods of play. Teams that played well during regular-season games
were invited to invitational and holiday tournaments.

The Kentucky High School Basketball Tournament is called
"the Sweet Sixteen" because Kentucky was then, as it is now, divided into sixteen regions going from west to east across the state,
with the first region being the Jackson Purchase. Each region is
subdivided into districts. District tournaments were, and still are,
set up by counties. The winner and the runners-up of each district
go on to the regional tournament, but only the winner of the
regional is invited to the state tournament.

Graves County had a total of nine teams in its district in the forties and early fifties but not that many now. Winners of the Graves
County District Tournament, as well as the runners-up, went to the
regional tournament played at Murray State University. Pairings in
the district and regional tournaments were drawn out of a hat or a

bucket in public by some person not involved in the tournament. Some districts in the past seeded teams and still do seed; that is, they have the coaches in a tournament meet and rate the teams. The No. 1 team is put (seeded) in the upper bracket and the No. 2 team is seeded in the lower bracket to improve the chances of having the two best teams meet in the finals. During Cuba's time, seeding was not done. Teams in the state tournaments have never been seeded.

In Kentucky's early days of basketball, before Cuba's heyday, high schools were classified as A, B, or C according to their enrollment. Despite the classification, the little schools were always allowed to compete against the large schools. That's why Cuba often played teams such as Louisville Manual, which had as many students in the senior class as Cuba had in its whole high school. Such pairings are rare today. School consolidations have for the most part swallowed up small Cuba-type schools, leaving fine private schools that attract students who are academically as well as athletically talented.

Some rules in basketball have changed and others have been added since Cuba's day. In the late forties and early fifties, there was no shot clock; a team in possession of the ball could hold onto it as long as it wanted without taking a shot. Also, you could formally practice as a team any time during the year, including summer months. Now teams can practice only during the regular season. Back then there was no limit on the number of years you could play on the varsity. If you were in the seventh grade and yet good enough to play on the varsity, you could play ball for six years. Today, you have only eight semesters of eligibility. Another change has to do with foul shots. Today, foul shots must be taken when a foul is committed. From 1945 to 1952, you could choose to take the ball out of bounds rather than shoot the foul shot.

Then, as now, a player has ten seconds to get the ball across the time (or half-court) line. The back court rule still applies in the sense that once the ball has been taken across the line, a player cannot go back across the line (even with one foot) unless the ball has been touched by a player on the opposing team and knocked or passed back across. Also, then as now, two officials refereed the games. Back then, though, you didn't get by with as much bumping as you do today. There was no three-second, lane-violation rule and no three-point arc.

If the teams were tied at the end of regulation play, they would play a three-minute overtime period. The first team to score, either by making a basket or a foul shot, won the game. This was called sudden-death overtime. If the teams were tied at the end of the first overtime period, they would continue to play sudden-death overtime periods until one scored. Today, if the score is tied at the end of the regulation time, the teams play a five-minute overtime period and the team ahead at the end of the overtime period wins the game. If the teams are tied at the end of an overtime period, the play continues into additional five-minute overtime periods until one period ends with a team ahead.

By Cuba's day, teams were no longer using a slow deliberate type of set-up offense that traditionally had resulted in low-scoring games. They were beginning to use a run-and-shoot type of basketball. Also, the two-handed set shot from the outside was beginning to be replaced by one-handed shooting. Defensively, teams used the all-court press a great deal, especially when behind in a game. Even the trap-zone press was beginning to be used in the 1950s. However, the jump shot did not come into prominence until late in that decade. There was much diversification as far as the kinds of defenses that were being played: zones, man-to-man switching back and forth, full-court press. The emphasis was on a running type of game—very exciting to play and to watch.

The college coach who made Kentucky the most exciting place in the nation to play and to watch basketball was Adolph Rupp, "the Baron of Basketball." The son of German immigrants who settled on a farm in southeastern Kansas, Rupp took charge of the Wildcats in 1930 and coached them until 1972, when he retired at the age of seventy. Under his guidance Kentucky won the National Collegiate Athletic Association championship in 1948, 1949, 1951, and 1958, and the Southeastern Conference championships twenty-seven times. Piloting Kentucky to 875 victories, Rupp was the winningest coach in collegiate basketball history until 1997 when Dean Smith, head coach of the North Carolina Tar Heels, surpassed Rupp's record and is now the all-time winningest coach with 877 victories.

Rupp insisted that running was the way to winning. He introduced the fast-break style of play, along with a set offense. He emphasized defense, especially man-to-man defense, saying repeatedly that "your defense will carry you through when your offense fails." He did not use a zone until the last half-dozen years of his tenure at UK.

Brash, flamboyant, and colorful in his mannerisms, speech, and behavior on the bench, Rupp was noted for his rough style of motivating players. He called them names that some of them had never heard before. He seemed to want everybody to hate him, and many did. His players either toughened to his insults and played the way he wanted them to play, or they quit. Dave Kindred, in his excellent book *Basketball: The Dream Game in Kentucky*, gives examples of Rupp's insulting behavior. Kindred writes that during one game, when Rupp was displeased with player Randy Noll's performance, he told Noll: "Are you writing home to your mother telling her you're not playing much basketball here at the university? Well, you —damned right. I don't know what it is you're playing, but it ain't basketball."

By 1946 Rupp's Wildcats were no longer dominating just the South; they were dominating the nation. While the Cuba Cubs were eighth and ninth graders just beginning to dream about the coveted state trophy, Rupp was leading Kentucky to its first national championship in 1948 and then again in 1949. In 1951 Kentucky became the first three-time winner of the NCAAs. The stars on that team were Bill Spivey, Frank Ramsey, Cliff Hagan, and Lou Tsioropolous. It was a great time to be a part of Kentucky basketball in any shape or form, and Coach Story and the Cubs basked in this era.

Kentucky did not have just one outstanding college coach, however; it had two. Ed Diddle was becoming a legend with his Western Kentucky State College Hilltoppers. Many think his best team was the 1948–1949 squad ranked among the top three in the nation—the University of Kentucky was number one! Diddle and

Rupp eventually were enshrined in the Naismith Memorial Basketball Hall of Fame.

High school basketball tournaments were just as exciting to watch as the college ones. Since its inception in 1918, the annual Boys' State Basketball Tournament has been the highlight of the athletic year in Kentucky schools. The first year the tournament was held at Centre College in Danville. Because the crowd was so large, however, the tournament games the following year were moved to the University of Kentucky gym in Lexington. Five years later, in 1924, continued growth in attendance forced another move of the state tournament to the larger new Alumni Gym in Lexington, where it stayed until 1941. But the ardent cage fans kept growing in numbers, and from 1945 through 1950 the Armory in Louisville was the site of the tourney. By 1951, the first year Cuba went to the state tournament, the 11,500-seat Memorial Coliseum in Lexington had just been completed and was the home of the championship for the first time. The games were played there until 1956 when they were moved to Freedom Hall in Louisville. The tournaments were then held alternately in the Coliseum and in Freedom Hall until the 22,000-seat Rupp Arena in Lexington was completed in 1976. Since 1995, they all have been played there.

The state tournament got to be such a rage in Kentucky that it became known as "March Madness" and "the Greatest Show on Earth." Shortly after World War II, gamblers zeroed in on the tournaments, making big money bets on high school teams. One night Clark County coach Letcher Norton pounded a guy and literally picked him up and threw him out of the gym after his players told him the man was trying to get them to shave points.

Two of the greatest high school basketball players of the late forties and early fifties were Cliff Hagan from Owensboro and Frank Ramsey from Madisonville. In the 1949 Boys' State Tournament, Hagan set a scoring record of forty-one points in the championship game, leading his Owensboro Red Devils winners past an outstanding Lexington Lafayette team. He and Ramsey went on to play for Rupp at the University of Kentucky, where, as sophomores, the two helped the Wildcats win the 1951 national championship. Then in 1954, as senior co-captains, they guided the Cats to an undefeated season, the first for UK since 1912. Both were All-Americans, and each had outstanding professional careers and the honor of being named to the Naismith Memorial Basketball Hall of Fame.

Among the many great high school players in those days were Wallace "Wah Wah" Jones of Harlan, Luther Risner of Hindman, Phil Grawemeyer and Ralph Beard of Louisville, Jerry Bird of Corbin, Sonny Allen and Frank Fraley of Breckinridge Training, Barney Thweatt of Brewers, Linville Puckett and Lewis Snowden of Clark County, and Phil Rollins of Wickliffe. In 1951 and 1952, Doodle Floyd, Howie Crittenden, and Jimmie Webb were added to the long list.

There were many great high school coaches, like Ralph Carlisle, who coached Lexington Lafayette into becoming the standard of excellence for the state; Letcher Norton, who led Clark County to hundreds of victories; Earl Jones, who started out coaching three years at Kavanaugh High School and then stayed twenty years at Maysville, winning 76 percent of his games throughout his twenty-seven-year coaching career. Also there was Lawrence McGinnis of Owensboro Senior High and S. T. Roach of Lexington Dunbar High. Roach led his all-black team to two state Negro championships and later was runner-up twice in the integrated state tournament. From small schools there was Russell Williamson of Inez, Oscar Morgan and Morton Combs of Carr Creek, and McCoy Tarry of Brewers.

During the 1947–1948 basketball season, Tarry's team from little Brewers won the state championship by beating Letcher Norton's Clark County, 55-48. That year Brewers' Redmen had the unique distinction of ending the season with a perfect record—the dream of every coach. Brewers is in the Jackson Purchase, in Marshall County, adjacent to Graves County on the east side.

The feisty, red-haired, freckle-faced Tarry was just a little over five feet tall; his feet didn't even touch the floor when he sat on some benches. But he was the hottest topic in western Kentucky, until Jack Story moved to Cuba.

CHAPTER 11

COACH STORY

"IN THE LONG RUN, MEN HIT ONLY WHAT THEY AIM AT."
—HENRY DAVID THOREAU

Graves County, Kentucky—1947–1948. The people in Cuba were thrilled to have Jack Story at their school again in 1947. When he had coached there once before during 1942–43, he brought the team the closest it had ever been to going to the state tournament. He led Cuba to the district runner-up position, losing by only one point to Benton. Both teams went on to the 1943 regional tournament, where Cuba again bowed out to Benton.

A quiet, imposing man with broad shoulders, Jack Story had an oval face and soft, wavy brown hair that he kept short and combed straight back without a part. He was an intense man, not a gladhander or backslapper. In speaking, he was direct, blunt; he meant just what he said. The people who knew him well said that he had a good sense of humor, that he appreciated a good joke even though he never told one.

As a coach and a teacher, he was a stern authority figure no one questioned. He got his point across without flattery or humor. He emphasized winning. He hated to lose and believed that playing for the sake of playing was nonsense. "Play to win! Put that ball in the hole!" he'd yell. His dark brown eyes could blaze with such an intensity that his ballplayers wished they could make themselves disappear. He was a stickler for details and a strict disciplinarian at school and at home. To a fearful student stammering excuses, "But, Coach, I'm, I'm, I'm tryin'," his response was, "I don't want you to *try*. I want you to *do* it." As a bench coach, he was a model of stoic control, never shouting to players or leaping up to berate officials. He thought coaches who let themselves get out of control were bad influences on their players. He would walk around at half court, during warm-ups, and talk to the players individually, putting them on guard, telling them to be alert and saying such things as, "Now, Doodle, you have not played against a guy like this Jerry Bird [from Corbin]. You're gonna learn something tonight, boy." Or he'd say, "Hell, Doodle, quit watching him play and *you* play!"

Story's mother, Lillian Bernice Emerson, was only seventeen when she gave birth to Jack on April 30, 1917, near the Story Chapel Church community in the southernmost part of Calloway County. She wanted to name her son John Boyd Story, but her husband, Leslie Abraham "L. A." Story, ten years older than she, insisted on naming the child Jack. A compromise of sorts took place: The infant was christened simply J. B., but called Jack. Both parents knew the value of education and eventually earned master's degrees. Lillian received two master's degrees, one from Murray State University and another from Wayne State University in Detroit.

L. A. Story taught in the area schools before becoming principal at the Pilot Oak school late in his career, so Jack attended

Cuba Coach Jack Story was a stern authority figure and a caring coach, although he did have a good sense of humor, too. (Cuba school yearbook photo)

81

several schools before he graduated from Almo, a high school then in Calloway County.

Beginning in his early childhood, Jack was interested in sports and played basketball at Almo, but he was always just a substitute. His coach, James "Baby" DeWeese, later became superintendent of Graves County schools and Jack's employer.

A good student, adept at mathematics and science, Jack graduated from Almo in 1933 when he was only fifteen. Knowing from the time he was small that he wanted to coach, he went straight to Murray State Teachers College in Murray, Kentucky, where he majored in physical education and math. He participated in boxing, basketball, and football at Murray, but he never starred in any of the sports.

By his junior year he ran out of tuition money and had to withdraw from college to find a job. At that time, 1935, a person could teach without having a college degree, and Jack took the first job offered to him—coaching at Fairbanks, a tiny community in Graves County only four miles from the Tennessee state line. The Fairbanks school had one teacher for all the lower grades, two teachers for the high school, and a total enrollment of thirty students. It had no gymnasium, just a dirt court behind the school, and no basketball team. Only ten boys were in the whole high school, including a Pentecostal who believed he'd suffer eternal damnation if he played any sports. One of the first things Jack did after he arrived at Fairbanks was pull a boy from the eighth grade in order to make a team, and next he nailed a basketball goal up in one of the large rooms upstairs. He wanted the boys to get all the practice they could shooting goals. As often as he could, he took them to the school in Sedalia where they practiced in the indoor gymnasium. "Remember," he told them, "the point of the game is for you to score and to keep your opponent from doing so." And score they did. In his first year coaching basketball at Fairbanks, Jack performed what was considered by many as a coaching miracle: He guided his team to winning the district tournament—the first and the only one in the history of that little school. The championship game was played in the old American Legion building in

Mayfield. Fairbanks's smashing victory over Mayfield, a large urban high school team, sent the Mayfield fans reeling in despair over what they believed was a humiliating defeat.

At the time his team won that game, Jack was only nineteen years old, younger than some of his players, for the age limit then for high school players was twenty. Despite his youth, he had uncanny ability to command respect and to teach his players how to enhance whatever natural ability they had. He had extraordinary understanding of the game and a desire to learn all that he could about it. He followed what other coaches were doing as closely as he could.

While Jack was coaching at Fairbanks, his dad was principal of the school at Pilot Oak, which at that time had an excellent basketball team. Called the War Horses, the team included James Austin, Tommy Ray, Red Garrigus, James Doyle Finley, Harold Vincent, Jack Olive, and Paul James Williams. When those boys earned their way to Pilot Oak's first Kentucky State Tournament in 1937, their parents and relatives raised enough money to buy their coach, Clovis Wallace, a suit and to pay for the team's travel and lodging expenses. L. A. asked Jack to go along to handle the money and act as team manager. The state tournament was unusual that year because in addition to Pilot Oak, there were several little schools competing, including Horse Cave, Hazard, Shady Grove, Midway, and Inez.

In the opening round of that 1937 tournament, Pilot Oak beat Breckenridge Training of Morehead, 30-27, but bowed out in the quarterfinals to Midway, 32-23. Midway went on to win the championship. That event left an indelible impression on Jack, who was so enthralled with the entire phenomenon of the state tournament that after attending that one, he never missed attending another, except the year he spent in the navy.

As he sat in Alumni Gym in Lexington that night in 1937 watching Midway receive the magnificent championship trophy, Jack was so struck by the magnitude of the ceremony he told the Pilot Oak boys sitting next to him, "I'm gonna come back here some day and win me one of those!"

83

Soon after he arrived at Fairbanks, Jack fell in love with Mary Lee Pittman, a slender, pretty, blue-eyed blonde student at the high school. After a brief courtship, they slipped away on June 14, 1936, to Paris, Tennessee, where they were married by a justice of the peace. They married without their parents' consent or knowledge. Afraid to break the news at first, each continued to live for a couple of weeks as they had before: Mary Lee at home with her parents and Jack in his rented room. But once their parents discovered the secret, they gave the young couple their blessings.

After Mary Lee graduated from high school in May 1937, she and Jack moved into a modest apartment in Murray so that he could finish work on his degree. Both got part-time jobs; she, as a waitress, and he, as an assistant to an electrician. On August 24, 1938, the first of their three children—Rex Daniel Story—was born.

After he received his bachelor's degree in 1939, Jack immediately went to work coaching at Centertown in Ohio County. After their second child, Carolyn, was born in 1940, he found it difficult to support his family on his meager salary. With two small children, Mary Lee was unable to work outside their home as she had done before. He loved his job, but the salaries for teachers and coaches were pitifully low in those days.

The rural areas of the Purchase did not have electric power in the early 1940s, so there were no industries to provide jobs. Many young people migrated to the industrialized North, hoping to find better lives, as Howie's and Doodle's older siblings and their fathers had done. Detroit was the mecca for poor Kentuckians in the late 1930s and 1940s. Likewise, Jack moved his family to Detroit in 1942, planning to work there long enough to save money to buy a reliable automobile and a home back in Kentucky. Then he figured that he could go back to coaching basketball, and Mary Lee could stay home with the children.

The young wife knew that basketball was at the core of Jack Story's identity. If she wanted to live with him, then basketball had to be an integral part of her life, too. As it turned out, she was the ideal wife for him. She molded her character and needs to suit his and helped him fulfill his dreams. She built her life around his. On nights out, they went to ball games, not to dinners or movies; their friends were avid basketball fans; their battery-operated radio was saved for listening to ball games; their extra spending money went to buy books and magazines about sports, coaches, and coaching techniques. He taught Mary Lee as much about basketball as he taught his team. At ball games, she kept the charts. As soon as each of their three children could follow the games and write, they helped her keep the charts.

After the United States declared war on Japan on December 7, 1941, and then four days later on Germany and Italy, our nation knew it was facing its greatest crisis. Expecting to be called into the military at any time, Jack did not want to leave Mary Lee and the babies in Detroit. So after just a few months in Detroit, he moved his family back to western Kentucky, where, in early 1942, economic conditions were just beginning to improve, thanks to the efforts of Graves County native Alben Barkley, then serving as majority leader in the U.S. Senate. Remembering the isolation and poverty of his childhood in Graves County, Barkley fought for improvements and electric power in all rural areas across the nation, especially in western Kentucky. He was instrumental in getting the high dams built on the Tennessee River and later on the Cumberland. With those dams, the Tennessee Valley Authority could provide many jobs for Purchase people, like Jack Story, who immediately got work as an electrician at the Shawnee Steam Plant on his return to Mayfield in 1942. The tourist business that gradually grew around the land between Kentucky and Barkley Lakes also provided employment, as did the two wartime defense plants that the federal government built in the Purchase.

One of these plants was at Viola, thirty miles outside of Mayfield. Also because of Barkley's influence, the Pennsylvania Salt Manufacturing Company was the first private industry to build a two-billion-dollar plant on the Tennessee River near Calvert City. But the Purchase people had been agrarian for so long, they found it difficult to become "industrialized." They resented the formalized management of unions and wanted to run them their own way.

85

Coach Jack Story and his wife, Mary Lee.
She knew hardly anything about basketball
when they married, but he patiently taught
her over the years, and she patiently
listened. (Photo courtesy of Carolyn Story)

Upon their return to Mayfield, the Storys found that life in
Graves County had changed dramatically because of the war. The
young men had left for the service. Many of the older ones had
moved north to work in defense plants. Women who had never
worked outside their homes were working now in the Mayfield
clothing factories—there were three by then, the Merit, the Curlee,
and the Andover—or at the new ammunition plant at nearby Viola.
Some of the older men worked at the defense plant too.

The Storys rented a small apartment in Mayfield. With the help
of an elderly neighbor lady who agreed to tend to the children,
Mary Lee went to work full-time as a presser at the Merit factory.
Although their life together was so uncertain, it was, for the time
being, more financially secure than it had ever been. In 1942, when
Jack was asked to coach at the Cuba school, he was reluctant to give

up his good-paying job as an electrician, but the thought of coaching basketball pulled his heart so strongly that he could not refuse.

He started work at Cuba in December 1942. By early 1943 the draft was including teachers and married men with children. Expecting to receive his call into the service at any moment, Jack left Cuba at the end of the 1943 school year and went to work for the Tennessee Valley Authority for over a year before entering the navy. He went to boot camp and school in Biloxi, Mississippi, but ended up serving only a brief stint before the war ended in the summer of 1945. After mustering out of the service, he worked in Saint Louis for a while before returning to Mayfield and his job as an electrician for the Shawnee Steam Plant. In 1947, when he learned that Kindred Winston was leaving the Cuba school, Jack applied for Winston's job and got it.

With three small children now, Jack figured he needed to continue working part-time at the Shawnee plant and signed on for a third shift three or four nights a week. Such a schedule allowed him to work at school all day until early evening or even later when he had ball games. Then he'd drive the ten miles home to Mayfield, get a couple of hours of sleep and a bite to eat, then drive thirty more miles to the plant where he worked until the early morning hours. Many a morning, he drove straight from the plant to the school without a chance to rest, change clothes, eat, or see his family. His schedule would have been fatal for someone who needed more than three hours of sleep each night, but he settled into it that fall of 1947 without any trouble.

Nearly every morning, he'd stop at Rhodes's general store to have a cup of coffee with the men who gathered there early each day. They'd talk about what Rupp's Wildcats were doing and how Diddle was making a big name for himself at Western. After his second cup, he'd leave so that he could be at school by the time the buses arrived. He taught civics and math classes in the morning, then coached the varsity basketball team and taught physical education in the afternoon.

CHAPTER 12

LITTLE CUBIE

"THESE WERE THY CHARMS—BUT ALL THESE CHARMS ARE FLED. SWEET SMIL-
ING VILLAGE . . . THY SPORTS ARE FLED, AND ALL THY CHARMS WITHDRAWN."
—OLIVER GOLDSMITH

Cuba, Kentucky—1946–1952. The closing of the Pilot Oak
high school brought Howie and Doodle together with Jack Story
and the other boys who would make the Cuba team, and it made the
little place with the strange name *Cuba* the center of their universe.

The orgin of the name of the little place obviously came from
the distant island. The connection between the Caribbean island of
Cuba and Kentucky's Cuba is rooted in the region's nineteenth-
century exportation of tobacco products. In the mid-1800s, before
the tobacco floors were established in Mayfield, farmers had to haul
their wagon loads of tobacco to the river closest to them. Southern
Graves County farmers hauled theirs to nearby Hickman, where the
Mississippi River flows into Kentucky. There they loaded their tobacco onto the packet boats to be taken downriver to New Orleans,
where an agent whom they had commissioned would sell it for them.

Conscious of their isolation, the farmers welcomed the men
who operated the packets, for they brought news from all the great
river towns—Memphis, Natchez, Vicksburg, New Orleans—and
from as far away as the British Isles and Spanish Cuba, too. The
farmers were aware of Cuba at that time for a couple of reasons. First
of all, Cuba was becoming one of their best customers, regularly

buying loads of Graves County dark tobacco to make its finest cigars, snuff, and chewing tobacco. Futhermore, Cuba was the center of a major national and political controversy in 1854, after U.S. expansionists threatened to take the island by force if Spain refused to sell it. Southern cotton farmers, especially, were hell-bent on acquiring Cuba as a territory. But the whole misguided idea of going to war for the island was so absurd that it was dropped, but not until after such intent had been widely publicized and heatedly debated.

Perhaps because they admired Spain's refusal to be bullied, or perhaps because the Cubans bought their tobacco, whatever the reason, in 1854 a group of Graves County farmers named their settlement Cuba. Note, too, that the other eight counties comprising the Jackson Purchase also have foreign place names, thus indicating the strong influence the outside world had on the area's settlers. There's a Paris, a Moscow, a Dresden, a Cadiz, a Feliciana, a Buena Vista, and a Dublin. One of the largest streams in Graves County is named Bayou de Chien, indicating the influence of the French explorers in the area. The locals' easy access to four great rivers—the Ohio, Tennessee, Mississippi, and Cumberland—provided Purchase farmers with the opportunity to engage in distant trade and to be aware of distant places.

From Mayfield, the county seat, Kentucky 303 drops straight south like a plumb line. If you follow it for about ten miles, you are in Cuba, only it was called "Little Cubie" around the time the Cubs were growing up. When you drove into Little Cubie back then, you'd have a sense of a very pleasant place—one that was steadfast and secure, where life was slow, where nobody ever got into a hurry. Nobody had anywhere to go. The people lived simple lives. They raised what they ate and made what they needed. Their motto was "Make it do or do without!" Except for their own spot of earth, the rest of the world could have fallen away and they would have survived. They were self-sufficient in a way that, perhaps, no one will ever be again.

In that age long gone, Cuba had a true sense of neighborliness. It was a closely knit community of people who were the descendants of those who had settled Cuba in 1852. They knew each other by first name. They looked after each other and swapped work. In the fall they got together to cut tobacco; in the winter, to kill hogs; in the spring, to get the crops planted. When it came time to thresh wheat, all the farmers and the one who owned a power-driven thresher would go from farm to farm until all the threshing was done. Whenever a man needed to build a house or a barn, his neighbors helped him. Nobody ever had to pay for labor, just for lumber and supplies. Oftentimes, the women and children would go along to prepare and serve huge meals, turning the workday into a social event.

Different levels on the social spectrum existed, but no one seemed to pay attention to them. A person's identity was earned, not inherited. A man was not judged by his ancestry or bank account, or lack of both. He was judged by how hard he worked, by how fair he traded, and by how well he got along with his neighbors and managed his business. If he could bind a hand of tobacco leaves quickly and beautifully, if he could train animals without being cruel to them, if he took pride in his place and kept it neat, if he was good to his family, if his children were well mannered and industrious, if he was honest—paid his debts and kept his word— a man was respected. These simple values were cherished and instilled in children. No one in Cuba ever felt a need to lock a door.

While the Cubs were growing up, Cuba had a blacksmith, a doctor, a school, two churches, two cemeteries, and two general stores. There was no courthouse, post office, cafe, bank, funeral home, sidewalk, stoplight, or jail. Cuba was never incorporated as a town. It never had a constable, magistrate, or sheriff; it didn't need one except on the rarest occasions. Then the sheriff from Mayfield came to take care of the problem. Cuba was not like that area around Dukedom, near the Tennessee line, where fussing, cutting, shooting, fighting, and drinking went on in the vicinity of a large moonshine still.

On those infrequent times when something went wrong, the Cuba folks were shocked, as they were on the day that Jim Taylor

Joe Buddy Warren, then nine, sports his new bike and straw hat in front of one of the houses in which he grew up. (Photo courtesy of Joe Buddy Warren)

died. For years there had been hushed talk about Pearl and Jim Taylor, who lived on the edge of the community. They were an odd pair who kept to themselves, never attending church, dinner-on-the-ground meetings, mule pullings, or basketball games. They seldom shopped at either store and never wanted anyone to visit them.

On the first cold morning in early winter 1942, Jess Warren and his son Joe Buddy were in the barn milking the cows by lantern light when Joe Buddy, nine years old at the time, noticed how bright orange the sky was over the field behind the school. Jess said, "Why, it looks like there's a fire over by Jim Taylor's house.

91

Run over by the school, son, and see if you can tell what's happening." Across the road from the Warrens' house and down another gravel road that led to Sedalia, the farmer Otis McPherson, his family, and neighbors were preparing to kill hogs that cold morning. They saw the flames, too, and stopped their work to run in the direction of the flames. As they were crossing the field, they met Pearl Taylor, bleeding badly from a cut skull.

She explained that earlier that morning, she and her husband had had "a terrible fit," and he struck her on the head with an axe handle. She passed out. Thinking that he had killed her, he must have panicked and set the house on fire. He ran to his barn where he apparently got a rope and then ran barefoot all the way down to the edge of his field, his bare feet leaving tracks on the frost-covered ground. When his wife came to, she saw the fire and ran for help. Meanwhile, her husband had climbed onto the split-rail fence next to a large persimmon tree. Standing on top of the fence, he looped one end of the rope around a tree limb and then around his neck. Then he jumped off the fence and hanged himself.

Following the footprints in the frost, Joe Buddy was the first to see Jim Taylor's thinly clad body dangling from the rope. As the boy stared, he did not realize that Ernest Copeland, a friend of his dad's, was standing behind him. When Ernest put his arm around his shoulder, the child screamed with terror and started running, thinking that Taylor's ghost had grabbed him. He ran smack into Otis McPherson, who held him tightly and spoke calmly to him, "There, there, son. It's all right."

Ernest climbed the fence and the tree and cut the rope. As the corpse dropped to the ground, it emitted a horrible groaning sound that sent another set of shock waves through Joe Buddy, causing him to scream.

But by the time school started that morning, Joe Buddy was something of a hero, hailed as the first to find Taylor's body. Kids clamored around him wanting to know all the gory details, which he was pleased to provide and with some embellishment.

The villagers gathered at the stores that morning to make arrangements to bury Taylor's body and to see to it that Pearl had a place to live.

Just about everyone who lived in Cuba or nearby came to the stores daily to trade, to get supplies, or just to talk. Talk was the main form of entertainment then.

Cuba's two general stores were built directly across from each other on the main road—Kentucky 303. Harper's, opened in 1936, was owned by Jack and Pauline Harper, whose daughter Barbara Ann was in the Cubs' class and one of the team's cheerleaders. Rhodes's was the oldest store in the village, dating back to the 1850s. It was a huge, white-framed, two-storied, boxlike building owned by Fred and his brother Carl, who had inherited it from their father, Mitchell Rhodes. There was no competition between the two store owners, and the village folk traded at both places. Everybody shopped at Rhodes's, though, because it carried everything.

Because of Barbara Ann, the children and their parents made Harper's their favorite hangout. Like Rhodes's, her dad's store had a real basketball goal. Depending on the weather, boys played basketball outside or checkers inside at both stores every day. Their critical and most vocal audience consisted of the store setters, the five or six near-octogenarians who sat at one of the stores all day, every day. In the summer they'd sit on the porches; in the winter, around the potbellied coal stove.

At the corner where Harper's stood, U.S. Route 83 intersected Kentucky 303 and wound around to the left of the store to the old Cuba school, a large, one-story brick building. The principal lived in the white frame house next door. The school was less than a mile and a half from the stores. Running back and forth between the school and the stores was part of the Cubs' training exercises.

The forerunners of the Wal-Marts, Kmarts, and Home Depots, these stores carried everything that anybody wanted or needed. They sold not only food but also clothes, hardware, seed, farm implements, building materials, saw blades, Octagon soap, bolts of colorful material and sewing notions, a few patent medicines, especially Lydia Pinkham's Vegetable Compound for Female Complaints. They carried what were considered delicacies—Arbuckle coffee, canned foods like salmon, sardines, tuna fish, and potted meat. Each store had a box for cold drinks, called "pop." Near the cash register, at a child's eye level, was a large glass jar full of candy. Against the walls were sacks of flour and cornmeal and wooden barrels of vinegar, sugar, and coal oil. The stores smelled of a potpourri of scents, from brine in the pickle barrel to licorice and peppermint sticks in the glass jars on the counter.

Doodle and Howie were practically inseparable when it came to playing basketball or checkers. Here they ponder their next moves at Harper's Store. (Photo courtesy of Charles Floyd)

The meat counters, kept cold with ice, held fat rolls of bologna, blocks of cheddar cheese, and sometimes fish. On top of the counter sat three big round glass jars, one filled with crackers, another with pickled eggs, another with pickled pig's feet. Bologna and cheese sandwiches were made to order.

On nights they were to play games, Doodle and Howie often stayed in Cuba instead of taking the bus home after school. They'd stay around the store, playing checkers, and then eat a bologna and cheese sandwich for supper. Doodle used to tease Pauline Harper at Harper's that she made her sandwiches so thin he got only one side of the bologna.

Gas pumps and dirt basketball courts were outside. Behind the stores were barns where chickens, hogs, eggs, corn, molasses, fresh vegetables, and anything else that had been brought in and traded for goods were stored. In those days farmers, for the most part, traded their fresh produce and dairy products. Cash came from the city folks from Mayfield, Murray, and Fulton, who came to shop in the country stores a couple of times a week.

During the 1940s rails in front of the stores and churches were used for hitching horses and mules, for there were still about as many wagons and buggies as there were cars and pickup trucks.

For decades the front yard at Rhodes's was the site of a makeshift post office built on a wagon wheel. Wooden boxes, nailed to the wheel, listed the names of the owners of the boxes painted in black. A welcome sight was the rural mail carrier who arrived weekday afternoons around two o'clock.

Twenty or so plain framed houses were on either side of the main road that ran through the village. A few other houses, at the ends of dirt roads, were miles apart from each other. Depending on the weather, the roads were either dusty, washboard rutty, or mud sloppy. Surrounded by large shade trees, some of the houses were built far back on their lots to avoid the dust. Nearly every house had a front porch with a swing. In the evenings folks sat on the porches or strolled over to the stores and visited there.

CHAPTER 13

THE DREAM BEGINS

"THE VERY ESSENCE OF LEADERSHIP IS THAT YOU HAVE TO HAVE A VISION.
YOU CAN'T BLOW AN UNCERTAIN TRUMPET."
—THEODORE HESBURGH

Cuba, Kentucky—Fall 1947. One afternoon just a few weeks after school started, Jack Story was in his classroom waiting for the lunch recess to end. It was a typical early October day, dry and still too warm to wear a jacket. The climate in the Purchase is like that in the South. His classroom was at the back of the school, and all windows were open. Noise from the playground drifted into the room.

A few minutes before the bell was to ring, Jack shoved the papers that he had been reading aside and walked from his desk to the window and looked out onto the playground. Some little girls were sitting under the shade of the tree with their lunch boxes scattered about on the ground. Another group was playing pop the rope; others were taking turns pushing and swinging on the makeshift swings made from old tires and ropes tied to the branch of the oak tree. Off to one side on the dirt basketball court, five skinny, shaggy-haired boys dressed in overalls and plow shoes were playing basketball. Their spirited improvisations captivated Story.

The tallest one of the five had astonishing natural ability to fake his passes to the smallest boy, who moved so fast as he dribbled the ball that he seemed to be floating above the ground.

96

The one faking the passes did so in such a comical manner that the others were giggling. One stocky kid could block and screen, while a feisty, sandy-haired fellow had an uncanny ability to jump with either foot and shoot. When the good-looking kid with the dark curly hair got the chance to shoot, he shot with an amazing accuracy from all over. All five boys handled the ball, shot, and moved with natural ability. As he watched them, Jack Story broke out into laughter, saying to himself aloud, "Well, I be damned."

A few days later after lunch recess, instead of meeting with his varsity, Jack met with the five eighth-grade boys he had watched on the playground. He shook hands with each one as they told him their names: The comic one who faked passes so well was Charles Kenneth Floyd, called "Doodle"; the small boy who dribbled the ball was Howard Crittenden, nicknamed "Howie"; the dark curly haired shooter was Jimmie Webb; the stocky blocker was Raymon McClure; and the feisty jumper was Joe Buddy Warren. Grabbing his straw hat from the hook on the wall, Coach Story led them outside the lunchroom, asking, "Say, are you guys interested in making a basketball team?" They looked up at him quizzically, shrugged their shoulders, and grinned. Pleased to no end that the coach was paying attention to them, they followed him out to the oak tree near the road that ran behind the school. He said, "Let's sit down here in the shade where it's cool and talk."

A large man, Story looked awkward as he bent down to sit on the ground. As he leaned back against the tree with his heavy legs crossed at the ankles, he loosened his tie and unbuttoned his collar. Howie and Doodle clamored to sit cross-legged on either side of him. As if he were thinking aloud to himself, Story began talking about basketball, about what it means to be a team, what it means compete, and what it means to win. He talked about what he called the "grandest sports event in the world"—the Kentucky Boys' Basketball Tournament, about how it was started in Danville in 1916 and later moved to Louisville and then to Lexington. He said that right from the start the monopoly on the title had been held by the big city schools—like Louisville Manual that had an enrollment of three thousand, or Lexington Lafayette with twenty-five hundred. He named other schools, names the boys had never heard of—Louisville Male, Saint Xavier, Owensboro High, Henry Clay, and Ashland Paul Blazer. In all those years, he emphasized, less than a handful of teams from unknown hamlets—like theirs—with high schools that had little more or fewer than a hundred students had ever won the championship. "But when those little places win, oh, their victories are so much sweeter." Then he surprised them by saying, "You know, it is not at all impossible for you to win the state tournament by the time you're seniors—if you start right now preparing yourselves to win."

The little boys were fascinated by all they heard, but they did not quite understand what he was telling them. They had never played on a basketball team, and no one had ever talked to them the way he was talking to them about basketball. They did not even know the rules of the game, and here this grown man—this coach—was telling them they could win the state championship when they got to be seniors.

Why, they had never even thought about being seniors, much less winning anything. What little they knew about basketball they had learned from watching their older brothers or other boys play in front of the stores. Except for a few occasions when their grammar school teachers had let them watch the varsity team practice or attend basketball games at school, they had not really seen many games.

All they realized that afternoon was that Coach Story loved to talk basketball, and he knew everything there was to know about it. He could name every team that had ever played in the state tournament, who their coaches were, and who scored what and why. He explained how the state is divided into many districts, and how the teams were placed in the districts.

The next afternoon Coach Story talked to the boys again. In this session he fell into his storytelling mode, talking about the time years ago, before any of the boys were even born, when little Carr Creek faced the mighty Ashland. Clear across Kentucky, on the opposite end of the state from us, he said, in the far southeastern corner in the Appalachian region of Knott County, an unknown little school called Carr Creek made basketball history in 1928. It was the first little school to work its way to the state tournament—an astonishing feat because Carr Creek had a total enrollment of forty-one students: twenty-three girls and eighteen boys. It had no gymnasium, no trained coach, no uniforms for the players, and no transportation for them, except horses and mules. The starters were all kin to each other; two were brothers and cousins to the other three. They had grown up playing basketball together and had played in all kinds of weather, usually on a dirt court on the side of a hill near the school. They walked or rode horseback miles to play in games in their area. But all the things that they did not have were offset by what they did have. Then, raising his hand, Coach Story struck each finger as he enumerated Carr Creek's strengths: They had natural ability, a love for the game, a willingness to work hard, an understanding of what it means to be on a team, and the will to win. Important also, he added, they had their community behind them.

Oscar Morgan, their coach, used to laugh and say that he didn't have to do much coaching. All he had to do was make the arrangements to play the games and chaperone. But, according to many old-timers who followed basketball keenly, Morgan was far too modest: He and his Mountaineers were the first to use the man-to-man court press that is so commonly used today.

In 1928 Kentucky's teams were separated into A and B categories, with the winner of each category meeting to compete for the state trophy. Carr Creek won the B championship by beating Lawrenceburg High, 37-11. Ashland won the A championship. When that happened, every basketball fan in the state wanted to see these two teams—the David and Goliath—play each other. According to John McGill, sports editor for the *Ashland Daily Independent*, "The largest crowd that had ever seen a high school game in Kentucky up to that time" attended that tournament game, while many hundreds were turned away.

At that 1928 tournament, Ashland, one of the largest schools in eastern Kentucky, was heavily favored when it met Carr Creek in the championship game. Yet Ashland struggled with Carr Creek's almost flawless man-to-man-defense. That game went into four overtime periods with Ashland making two more free throws than Carr Creek and barely winning, 13-11. The newspapers reporting the game called attention to the fact that Carr Creek had played straight through the district and the regional tournaments without calling a time-out and without committing a single personal foul.

The score was so low, Coach Story explained, because of "stalling" or "freezing" the ball—a tactic used to protect a lead. When a team got a few points ahead, it would try to hold on to the ball by passing and faking plays, or both, unless a player had an irresistibly good shot or a free throw. The rules in those days set no time limit on how long a team could hold the ball by passing or by dribbling it. They could keep it until the clock ran out. For teams with excellent dribblers and passers, this method provided an ideal way to keep the other side from scoring. Once a team got ahead in the last quarter, it would play keep-a-way with the ball. If a player in possession of the ball was fouled during this time, he had a choice of doing one of two things: He could take the free throw or he could keep possession by taking the ball out of bounds. Then he could run the time out so that the other team would not have a chance to score.

Although Carr Creek did not win the championship, Coach Story chuckled, "They put up a helluva fight." They were outstanding enough to get invited to go with Ashland to Chicago to participate in the 1928 National Invitational High School Basketball Tournament, held annually after the state tournaments. For a while it looked as if the two Kentucky teams would play each other again in the national finals. But after winning three games, Carr Creek lost to a team from Georgia, a team that Ashland beat in the final game. So Ashland won the national title. But Carr Creek got just as much, if not more, national publicity. Coach Story smiled, saying, "Just goes to show you, the size of the school doesn't have

100

anything to do with the winning. It's how determined the team is to win." Carr Creek exemplified the kind of determination that Story wanted to inspire in those little boys.

All coaches have their own methods of motivating their players; they have their favorite words and language. And Coach Story's favorite word was *determination.* He applied it to every human endeavor. "You listen here," he'd say. "Nobody gets anywhere unless he's determined to get someplace. Nobody's going to give you anything either. Don't be thinking they are. You can't just have a dream and sit back expecting it to happen. Fools do that. You've got to work to make a dream happen. And work hard, too. What some call 'good luck' is nothing but the result of hard work. You don't win by luck, you win by working." He had already seen in them a strong spirit of competition, and he wanted to encourage that spirit. "Now, it'd be nice for us to win the regionals— that's a dandy honor for any little place like ours. But," he paused and leaned forward, whispering confidingly, "winning the state basketball tournament is the grandest honor in the world."

Before they left school that day, those little boys believed that they would bring that honor home to Cuba by the time they were seniors. They were inspired by their coach's dream. They were his most ardent audience, and Coach Story never let up with his talk of their winning the championship. With that goal in mind, the boys had from the start a good reason to win every game they played. They didn't know it, but Jack Story was obsessed with the idea of coaching a championship team. Many a night when he wasn't working his shift at the plant, after his wife and children had gone to sleep, he'd sit at his kitchen table drinking coffee, going over and over the stats. He'd think about the next day's practice sessions or the last game his team played and try to figure out why mistakes were made in a game or in a practice. He scouted games, spotted players, learned new techniques, and kept shot charts. Mary Lee would wrap the children up warmly, and they would all go with Jack in their old Plymouth to some basketball game as far away as thirty or forty miles.

101

Coach Story read all the books about basketball that he could lay his hands on and pored over the sports pages in the daily newspapers. He followed the progress of other high school coaches and his idols—Rupp and Diddle—who were earning immortality coaching basketball. He acquired films from Rupp that he watched over and over. During the 1947–48 season, Rupp was coaching what became known as the Fabulous Five: Ralph Beard, Alex Groza, Wallace "Wah-Wah" Jones, Cliff Barker, and Kenny Rollins (the floor leader for the five), and alternates Dale Barnstable, Joe Holland, Jim Line, Jim Jordon, Roger Day, and Garland Townes. This group outscored their opponents in the 1948 season by an average of 24.6 points a game and ended the season with a 36-3 record. They won the University of Kentucky's first National Collegiate Athletic Association basketball championship in 1948 and went on to compete in the Olympic Games in London, England, where the U.S. team won a gold medal. Basketball was—and is—king in Kentucky.

CHAPTER 14

PREPARING TO WIN

"NOTHING IS ACHIEVED BEFORE IT IS THOROUGHLY ATTEMPTED."
—SIR PHILIP SIDNEY

The Cuba School—Spring 1948. Malleable and eager to learn, the eighth-grade boys provided Jack Story with all the raw material he needed for a championship team. His own determination to mold them into athletes soon became evident. Every day after lunch he'd talk to them for a while and then put them to work learning fundamentals of the game. As long as the weather permitted, they practiced outside because the varsity used the gym. The boys had a cooperative spirit and wanted badly to please Coach Story.

Although he encouraged each boy to develop his own strength and to try out for the position he felt most comfortable playing, Coach Story demanded that each learn the basic moves of all the other positions. He explained that natural ability is a blessing for any would-be athlete, but the blessing has to be combined with a thorough knowledge of the fundamentals of the game. "Learn the fundamentals," he preached.

Howie and Joe Buddy were short and fast and were inclined to run the court, dribble, and shoot. They were natural guards. Doodle, the tallest among them, was a pivot, center, passer, and shooter. Jimmie, who was nearly as tall as Doodle, was a natural forward who knew how to keep the ball high at shoulder level and to move fast. He could rebound and score remarkably well. Raymon was a great rebounder and blocker. In practice sessions, however, Coach Story had them play different roles. Every afternoon from 12:30 until school let out at three, they practiced dribbling, passing, faking, learning which foot to jump off and why, ball handling, and shooting. Coach Story hammered at them about shooting. Each player had to be an excellent shooter, and he meant "excellent" while being closely guarded. He'd give them an assignment and then leave them to practice it while he went inside the gym and worked with the varsity. Before he left he warned them, "Don't do anything in practice that you wouldn't do in a game."

As the passing of years would later show, Jack Story was ahead of his time in his coaching techniques. He valued each player's uniqueness and his boys knew that. Each player learned the basic moves of all the positions while developing his own uniqueness. Unlike other coaches at that time, Jack Story did not have all the players on the floor during practice learning the same technique at the same time. He allowed them to experiment, to develop their natural inclinations to jump, shoot, dribble, and guard. He told them repeatedly he wanted them to have fun playing basketball and to love playing.

Under Coach Story's direction, Howie developed into an extraordinary keep-a-way dribbler who could maintain possession of the ball for minutes at a time.

Doodle's weird, winding windmill shots contradicted the tried-and-true methods of shooting. Yet Doodle won many games for the team using this peculiar shooting style. Perhaps if some other coach had seen Doodle as an eighth grader getting ready to make one of his signature shots, that other coach would have stopped the boy immediately and retrained him to shoot according to the accepted style of the day.

By all standards of reality today, the Cubs' dream of winning the state championship would have seemed absurd. It wasn't to them. They had a coach who loved basketball and knew all there was to know about it, a coach who was interested in them and wanted to teach them what he knew about the game. The Cubs loved basketball as much as the coach did, and Howie and Doodle especially loved it. After regular practice every afternoon, they would play one-on-one on the dirt court in front of Wagoner's until supper time. After supper they'd rush through their chores and then get together again to play some more until dark. When the moon was full, providing the light they needed, they played late into the night. Whenever Howie and Doodle were separated, they practiced alone. Not understanding their sons' passion for the game, their fathers whipped them soundly more than once for, as the fathers said, "foolin' with that basketball all the time" instead of working.

One time when Howie was dribbling the ball in front of the store, a stranger stopped to buy some gas. He was traveling through to Fulton, Tennessee. After watching Howie for a few seconds, he told him: "You are really good at handling that ball. You are *really* good to be so young." Howie was thrilled by the stranger's compliment. Having the old men at the store hear what he heard made Howie even happier.

Jack Story knew early on that Howie and Doodle had the most star potential among the players. He also knew that they were the sons of sharecroppers who didn't always make ends meet no matter how hard they worked. Although the parents of the other boys were not well off, they all had jobs in addition to their farming, jobs that provided a small but steady income. Sharecroppers never had a steady income. They had nothing to count on—not the weather, not the crops, not the landlord who could make life even harder for them. Sharecroppers were the poorest of the poor. Yet the children were not aware of their poverty; the custom of equality prevailed in Graves County. But Jack Story was sensitive to it. He paid both boys for doing jobs around the school, such as painting the cafeteria and the hallway. In the summers during their last two years in high school, he got them jobs at the Pet Milk Company. He knew that if he helped them get athletic scholarships to colleges, the colleges would open the doors to the outside world for them. He expected them to work hard at basketball and at their schoolwork, even though the demands he made on their time might have suggested otherwise. Still, their high school education was essential to their success in college work. No college coach wants a boy who is unable to make his grades and therefore unable to maintain his eligibility.

During one of his early pep talks, Coach Story tried to foster a spirit of competition: "Winning requires hard work. If you work hard, you can make your life better. Another thing, you can set your mind just like you can set a clock. Setting your mind is important." He stood up, put his big hands on the back of the chair, and leaned toward them, saying huskily: "Now you guys listen to me. God gave each of you some ability. You can waste it, or you can perfect it. You perfect it by practicing, and practicing means work. Of course, it's a lot easier to work if you've got a goal in mind!"

As Jack Story stood staring out of the smudged windowpane at the gravel road that ran in front of the school, the little boys, dressed in double-patched overalls, faded shirts, and hand-me-down plow shoes laced with binder twine, gathered around wondering what he was thinking. After a long silence, he told them: "Look down the road. What do you see? You can't see very far down that road, can you? But you can go pretty far down it if you want to. You can go to Sedalia or Pilot Oak or Water Valley or Mayfield—or to Paducah, even to Nashville or to Detroit. That sounds pretty far to you now, doesn't it?" he chuckled. "You can get on that road and go all the way to Lexington. And far, far beyond if you've got the gumption to go." He looked down at their upturned faces and concluded quietly, "Just takes hard work and determination! You hear me? Hard work and determination."

Young as they were, they did not understand him fully, but they understood him enough to want the same things he wanted. And to them, what Coach Story wanted was fun. Getting out of class and study hall every afternoon to practice basketball was more fun than they had ever imagined they'd have at school. Eager to please him, they worked diligently to improve their skills.

Until Jack Story came into their lives in the autumn of 1947, those kids had had no one to talk to them about how important it is to have a dream. No one had ever talked to them about setting goals and working step by step to achieve them. And the idea of being "honored" for doing what they loved—playing basketball— was hardly believable. All their parents had ever done was complain about their ball playing. All their parents ever talked about was getting the crops in and out, feeding the livestock, milking the cows, cleaning the fence row, and praying that enough would be made from the tobacco to get them through the winter. They weren't the kind of people who talked about achieving success and certainly not by playing basketball. Many didn't even know that athletic scholarships were available to help their youngsters get into and through college. Just getting through the day was challenging enough for them. Although they were hard workers, some much more so than others, few of them had any real ambition.

Every afternoon Coach Story worked with the boys, explaining to them what it meant to be an athlete. "You play fair. You never cheat. You win by outplaying your opponent, by making more points, by being better than he is. Don't ever go into a game thinking that you're in for an easy time. It's dangerous to underestimate the other side. And don't ever let me hear you talk back to a referee. If you lose, you lose like a man." He harped constantly on how important it was that they work hard to improve themselves. He gave countless examples of individuals and of teams who had overcome great odds and succeeded. He also taught them how important it was to take good care of themselves, and he made them feel very grown-up when he handed each a jock strap and explained the value of wearing one. He insisted that they dry their necks and backs well after sweating or showering to avoid catching colds, but he warned them against washing their hair with hot water, saying, "That'll make it fall out!" He told them how important it was to get plenty of rest. He showed them how to hold the basketball with their fingertips rather than with the palms of their hands so it wouldn't slip. He taught them a way to bend their thumbs back to strengthen their wrists and urged them to practice this exercise while sitting in class listening to their teachers.

After watching them walk and run, he scolded, "Now if you guys want to be ball players, you'd better stop walking like one-legged ducks. You got to learn to walk right, so you'll run right. Don't run slew-footed! You lose some of your power if you don't push off with your toes." During their first practice session on that dirt road behind the school, all they did for two hours was walk with their toes pointed straight.

At the next practice session, he explained: "Remember! Your objective in basketball is to throw the ball through the hoop. Your opponent's objective is to prevent you from doing that. So in order to get a decent shot, you've got to fool him. You've got to make him think you are going one way when you're really going another way. You've got to learn lots of ways to fake him. You can fake with your hands, your head, your waist, your legs, and with your eyes." Then he'd throw the ball without looking in the direction he was throwing it and hit one of them, purposely startling the unsuspecting human target to make his point. Next he'd call one of the boys onto the court with him to demonstrate some faking techniques. After his demonstration, he'd leave them to practice faking for an hour or so.

Coach Story devised simple ways of teaching them how to pass, shoot, dribble, and rebound. One of his shooting drills was to have them put one hand in their back pocket and shoot with the other. Then he would have them switch hands. For hours on end, he made them dribble through an obstacle course of wooden chairs. He would set a chair at the free-throw line and make the boys dribble up to it. They had to go up straight for a jump shot without banging into the chair. One afternoon while they were scrimmaging in practice, Jimmie Webb threw a pass that accidentally hit Coach Story in the head as he sat on the bleachers. "I thought for sure I'd be killed or sent home," Jimmie said. "But he said nothing to me. Just went on like nothing had happened." Unintentional mistakes like that one, he ignored.

Coach Story arranged for them to play other eighth-grade teams in the area; then he held intramural tournaments, pitting these eighth graders against the ninth graders and even the tenth graders. When they beat the other eighth graders and the ninth, he grinned, knowing that his championship team was blooming. Although they hungered for praise, he rarely gave it to them. He was never demonstrative, but they quickly got to the point where they could read his face. They knew by the way he watched them play that they were doing well. Pleasing him made them feel good.

He convinced them that their preparation routine required doing some tedious tasks repeatedly each day. If they were going to win the championship, they had to prepare themselves to win. Using the dirt road behind the school, he trained the boys to develop their peripheral vision. He taught them to walk holding their heads and backs straight, pointing their toes straight, while they stooped to pick up handfuls of rocks to throw from behind their backs at trees. He wanted them to learn to see without looking, to hit those trees without turning their heads in the direction they were aiming.

Howie, by far, was the most conscientious about practicing everything Coach Story instructed. Without question, Howie was committed to being the best he could be. He practiced every skill longer and more attentively than Doodle and all the others put together. After Coach Story told the boys to walk straight, Howie walked straight everywhere he went thereafter. Because his family had no car, he had plenty of opportunities to practice his walking. People in Pilot Oak were amused when they first noticed the boy practicing. No taller or wider than a bed slat, fifteen-year-old Howie would walk along the road by himself ramrod straight. Holding his head high, he'd throw rocks from behind his back, hitting trees one right after another as he went along. The villagers thought he was a sight to watch. Born with superb eye-hand coordination, Howie loved and mastered this exercise. Even while he was in the classroom, he practiced seeing without looking at who was on either side of him, and he knew what each person was doing. He developed exceptional peripheral vision, an ability that gave him a great advantage coming down the court on a fast break. He could run down the court and know where all the players were and what they were doing without looking at them. Such court sense is rare among basketball players.

As ninth graders, the team had to practice every afternoon from 12:30 to 3:00 and then ride the bus home. After the bus let Howie and Doodle out at the store in Pilot Oak, the two of them would get the basketball from Mr. Fred and play in front of the store until suppertime. They were becoming such good players that the older boys looked forward to playing basketball with them. Because Doodle had a three-mile walk home, he didn't get to play as late as Howie, who lived just across the street from the dirt court. Unless his mother allowed him to spend the night with the Crittendens, Doodle would have to run the three miles home in order to arrive before his dad came in from the fields. If Vodie had known then that Lexie was doing their son's chores so that Doodle could play ball in front of Wagoner's, Vodie would have been furious. Those times when Doodle did not get home early enough, Vodie would be angry. He sincerely believed that his son's ball playing was a sign of shiftlessness and irresponsibility. Nevertheless, Doodle withstood his father's whippings and lectures and kept playing basketball.

He and Howie played in all kinds of weather; even in the winter they'd be out in front of the store playing with their hats, coats, gloves, and boots on. It was sometimes so cold their hands would hurt handling the basketball, bouncing it off the frozen ground. Then as the ground thawed, it would get so muddy that they had to wear working boots in order to play. They'd slip, slide, and fall in the mud, laughing. Their basketball, clothes, and hands would get muddy, but that didn't stop them from playing.

When it was raining or sleeting, they sneaked into the Pilot Oak school and used one of the team's basketballs. Even though the old gym really wasn't any good, the principal, Mr. Douglas, still refused to let Howie and Doodle practice in it. While Howie was in the sixth grade, however, he had discovered a way to get into the gym secretly. By standing on Doodle's shoulders, Howie could reach a windowsill, remove a loose pane on a window, and crawl his way through the opening. Once he was inside the building, he'd unlock the back door for Doodle. Within seconds, they would have a good basketball and the whole gym to themselves. In the winter, the old place was freezing cold; in the summer, boiling hot; but they played regardless of the temperature.

In the summertime with his windows open, Mr. Douglas, who lived next door to the school, would hear the ball bouncing in the gym and run them off. But his threats never deterred them from continuing to break into the school every time they could. They never stole or bothered or damaged anything in the school; they just played basketball in the gym. Sometimes they posted a younger kid as a lookout to warn them if Mr. Douglas was headed their way. The only time they ever got scared was the time the candy closet at school had been broken into. They were worried sick that they would be accused of the crime. Although they were not, that event did not scare them enough to stay out of the gym.

Howie and Doodle were unique among the boys on the team because they were competitive with each other. They motivated and challenged each other constantly. When just the two of them were playing ball, they'd argue about playing full court or half court. Howie liked to play a full-court basketball game because he was fast and could beat Doodle every time. Doodle liked to play a half court game where he had the advantage with his height. They argued which way they were going to play first and then they'd play a game each way.

Coach Story gave them an old basketball that was slightly ripped. All the air was out of it, and it couldn't be puffed up. So in their usual custom, the boys stuffed it with rags and made it do. They couldn't bounce it, so they just kept passing it back and forth, sometimes for half a day, as they ran up and down the dirt road between Pilot Oak and Water Valley. In the winter, they prayed the ground would stay frozen so that they could continue to play outside.

CHAPTER 15

THE HARLEM GLOBETROTTERS IN CUBA

"WE ARE SUCH STUFF AS DREAMS ARE MADE ON."

—SHAKESPEARE

The Cuba School—1948–1949. One cold rainy afternoon in late 1948, Coach Story abandoned the usual practice session and took the ninth-grade team of basketball prodigies into the auditorium, where a film projector was set up. Facing them, he sat straddled in a straight wooden chair with his hands on his knees and said confidingly, "There are two secrets to this game. One, you've got to learn to move with the ball the way you move without the ball. And two, you've got to learn to fool your opponent. You've got to make him expect anything except what you are really going to do. Now, watch this film and you'll see what I mean."

Coach Story turned out the lights and started the projector, which summoned flickering images of the Harlem Globetrotters. The little boys scooted to the edges of their wooden chairs astonished by what they saw—agile men dribbling and handling the ball like magicians. Playing marvelously dexterous tricks with the ball, making improbable goofy wonderful shots, they were having a glorious time. In that darkened room in that tiny rural school, a hand-

112

ful of farm boys went wild with glee. When the film was over, they begged to see it again, and Coach Story obliged. That film was a revelation to them. The only basketball they had ever seen was the orthodox games played by the schools in their area. This one was a game they had never seen before—creative, embellished, and showy.

After they watched the film a second time, Coach Story told them, "Now, you go into the gym and practice what you saw the Globetrotters doing." Talking and laughing, they leaped from their chairs and ran into the gym. Now they had a vision to go with their own experience.

Doodle's older brother Bill had seen the Globetrotters play in Detroit and had told Doodle about them and Goose Tatum's hook shot. He even tried to show Doodle how it was done. Until he saw Goose Tatum play, Doodle never understood what Bill was talking about. But once he saw Goose Tatum in action that day, he knew exactly what the steps were.

Tossing an imaginary ball, Doodle and Howie ran down the hall faking and darting around each other. Doodle started imitating Goose Tatum; Howie, Marques Haynes.

Every chance they got, the ball players went into their Globetrotters' act. Martha Layne Casey, who was in the Cubs' class, lived in Pilot Oak. She often saw Doodle and Howie running up and down the road past her house in the late afternoons, pretending they were Tatum and Haynes. Doodle had a terrific crush on her, mainly because she was utterly unattainable. While other girls were swooning around Doodle, Martha kept her distance. Her attentions were focused on Jimmie Webb, who was so shy he could not look her in the eye. Determined to sway her affections, Doodle believed his and Howie's basketball act of dribbling, darting around each other, and faking moves—without a basketball—would impress her. However, she was more amused than impressed. She laughed as she watched the tall boy bend over and wave his long arm up in the air, practicing his hook shot with his invisible basketball while Howie guarded him. Despite Doodle's efforts to attract her, Martha never wavered from her affection for Jimmie.

When Jimmie Webb first met Martha Casey, he was so shy he could barely look her in the eye. That had changed by the time they graduated, as shown here the day after their graduation from Cuba. (Photo courtesy of Jimmie Webb)

Coach Story decided to use Howie and Doodle, as ninth graders, on the varsity team. But Howie was so small that they had no uniform to fit him. The coach's wife had to cut an old uniform down, and even then, it was still too large.

The first varsity game Howie participated in was during the Purchase Pennyrile Tournament at Murray. The game was held in the old Carr Health Building on the campus of Murray State Teachers College. Cuba was playing Nortonville and trailing. Somebody passed Howie the ball. He was in such a panic that as soon as he got it, he turned and tried to pass it right back to the same player who had turned away from him. Nervous, Howie threw the ball—hitting the player smack dab in the middle of his back. When he realized what he had done, he sank to the floor and covered his face with shame.

Early on, Doodle did not fare much better. In his first game as a varsity player, against Wingo, he made four fouls in the first minute. He was so upset, he ran over to the coach, pleading to be taken out. Coach Story said, "Hell, it won't take you long to get that other one. Go back in!"

In his first game, Jimmie Webb was so nervous when he got the ball that he dribbled down the other end of the court and scored a basket for the other side.

During games Coach Story sat still on the bench with both feet flat on the floor, his arms straight and close to his body with the palms of his hands flat on the bench. He leaned forward sometimes, but he never stood up and never yelled. He knew that the look on his face revealed all that he felt and ordered them: "If you make a mistake during a game, don't look at me! Just keep on going." During the warm-ups, he also insisted that his players never look down the court at their opponents. "Makes you look like you're dreading them."

As ninth graders, the Cubs grew stronger and Coach Story played them against other junior-varsity teams. Their first out-of-town game was against older, more experienced ninth graders at Beadleton. The Beadleton gym was upstairs and had six posts on the ball court, three on each side. The ceiling was so low that the top of the backboard touched it. The Cubs couldn't put an arc on their shots and couldn't get used to driving around the posts. They lost by six points. Coach Story was very unhappy and on their ride home, he shamed them by saying, "Well, I guess I was wrong. I thought you boys were going to be ball players."

After Beadleton he drilled them even harder on the fundamentals of the game. He taught them how to throw a pass, catch a pass, shoot a ball, and time a rebound. He had them dribble through a maze of chairs for hours. He taught them to guard a player by watching his beltline and feet to predict which way he would move. "But watch the guy's eyes, too, because he might signal with them." Also, he insisted that they talk to the players they were guarding: "Say anything that will distract him!" Doodle perfected this tactic to the point where he sometimes made his opponent break out in laughter. One time much later, just before a game with Wickliffe was to begin, Doodle told opposing player Phil Rollins, "You're so wonderful. I got a picture of you on my bedroom wall." The surprised Rollins burst out laughing as he ran down the court.

Coach Story also encouraged the boys to experiment with the game. He was silent about their flashy moves, and behind-the-back passes that didn't always connect. He didn't mind their trying unusual shot-making techniques or their failed attempts. Unlike other coaches, he allowed them to ad lib on the court. He never tried to make them conform to a certain way of playing. Whenever he saw that they were getting too tense in practice, he would have them stop practicing for three days. He never wanted them to play mechanically or by rote. He wanted them to be creative and relaxed while playing—to love playing and to have fun.

The boys were at times mischievous in class, especially after they realized how important they were to Coach Story. But none of them was a whiner or a laggard. They were all motivated to excel, and they viewed Coach Story as an unquestioned authority. His obsession for basketball became their obsession. His desire for excellence became theirs.

During their after-school one-on-one sessions, Howie and Doodle developed skills on their own. Without any instruction from Coach Story, they perfected different plays by practicing in front of Wagoner's. By the time they had completed the ninth grade, they had played together for so long that each knew precisely where the other would be on the court in a game. For one thing, Doodle, the center, and Howie, a guard, learned to make perfect blind passes. Howie would throw the ball to Doodle and then cut right across in front of Doodle and run to the basket. Doodle would fake as if he were going to shoot a hook shot or pass the ball to somebody else. All the while Doodle knew exactly where Howie was going and would make a blind pass to him.

On a rebound shot, Doodle would tip the ball out to the side.

Howie would know which way Doodle would tip the ball from where he was on the court and would position himself to catch it. Then the two of them would be off and gone on a fast break. When their opponents shot a free throw and missed, the Cubs would tap the ball to the side, and Joe or Howie would go get the ball, turn, look for a man running down the court, and hit him in the middle of the court. Then they would be on a fast break again.

By the beginning of the tenth grade, Doodle was four or five inches taller than any of the others on the team except Harold Roberts. He was so thin the old store setters said that they had to spin him around in the shower to get him wet. He was so tall that his elbows, sharp as blades, would catch teammates in the eyes and nose. Some of their practice sessions got rough. During these sessions, they'd play half court only. Ted Bradley, would guard Howie; Bill Pollock, Raymon; Paul Simpson, Joe Buddy; Jimmy Brown, Jimmie Webb; "Tennessee Harold" Roberts, Doodle. Harold and Doodle played so roughly with each other that they stayed bruised and sore. Doodle's nose was broken once and another time Harold's was. Doodle didn't go to the doctor about his broken nose. He liked it beaked up and thought it gave him a more rugged, cowboyish look.

As they got older, all—except Howie and Doodle—developed interests outside of basketball. Joe Buddy and Ted liked to bird hunt and fish in Patterson Lake. They rigged up some fishing and hunting equipment and struck out on their own during their free time. Both had girlfriends, and by then Joe Buddy and Ted took turns driving their dads' cars on double dates. After Jimmie Webb got past his shyness and started talking to Martha Layne Casey, he wanted to be with her every waking hour. Raymon had fallen in love, too, with a girl who lived in Sedalia, and he wanted to be with her as often as he could. In fact, he married her at the beginning of their junior year in high school. The only two who were wholeheartedly devoted to basketball were Doodle and Howie. Howie was far more dedicated than Doodle; Howie gave 100 percent of his effort; Doodle gave about 80 percent. Although both had girlfriends, too, they didn't let them interfere with their basketball.

CHAPTER 16

PRIDE COMETH

"OF ALL THE ANIMALS, THE BOY IS THE MOST UNMANAGEABLE."
—PLATO

The Cuba School—1949–1950. Because he was larger than the others, Doodle thought he was more mature than he actually was as he entered his sophomore year. When the little row of fuzz above his upper lip had grown darker and thicker, he started smoking cigars publicly and skipping classes to hitchhike to Mayfield to play pool with some older boys. But no matter what his mornings were like, he always appeared at the school in time for lunch and stayed for afternoon basketball practice. Sometimes he could slip into the gym through the back entrance without Coach Story realizing that he had been absent all morning. The gym was in the center of the school building and had classrooms on both sides; study hall was at one end and Coach Story's office was at the other end, near the front of the building.

After Mrs. Warner, the English teacher, informed Coach Story that Doodle and a couple of others on the team were failing her class, the coach told the boys that they had to pass to stay in school, and they had to stay in school to play basketball. More than anything else in the world, Doodle wanted to play basketball; the court was his stage. Playing ball made him feel happy, respected, and admired. Although he knew he was good and that the coach needed him, he was still afraid that he was going to get suspended. At that point one of his classmates, Donald Poyner, came to his rescue. A small, slightly built boy with dark hair and dark brown eyes, Donald was nicknamed "Central Intelligence" by his peers because he was intellectually and academically ahead of his classmates and even some of his teachers and also because Coach Story funneled some of his own professional duties to Donald. In fact, years later, the community was surprised to learn that it was Donald who sometimes ran the school while the principal was preoccupied with coaching.

An only child, Donald was well adjusted, confident, and mature beyond his years. His intelligence was acknowledged throughout the Cuba area. One story concerning him and one of the old men who sat at Rhodes's had to do with a set of *World Book* encyclopedias the boy received for Christmas 1947. Often a visitor in the Poyners' home, the old man noticed the boy's reading habit. One day when someone at the store commented about how smart Donald was and about his ability to do such and such, the old man announced, "That boy oughta be smart. He's got his head stuck in dem sac-a-peters all the time."

Donald offered to tutor Doodle, and any others, too. As class president, Donald mobilized the class, all thirty-four students. He talked about the Cubs' goal and urged the class to share the Cubs' dream of winning the state championship. Each student agreed to help. By Thanksgiving the tenth graders were organized: the girls were either cheerleaders, members of the pep squad, or tutors. The boys were players, managers of the team, or tutors. The tutors' job was to make sure that all the homework was done correctly and turned in on the day it was due. They also scheduled study periods before tests. Several courtships began among the class members around this time as the tutors fell in love with the "tutor-ees." For instance, Martha Layne Casey was in love with Jimmie Webb, who also adored her. She saw to it that his work and hers were done to perfection. Doodle, smitten by pretty Julia Harris, wanted her for a tutor, not Donald. But Coach Story told him, "Put that idea out of your mind."

During the 1949–50 basketball season, the Cubs put together an impressive string of victories over all the schools in Graves County,

119

which were the only ones they played. Although they were making a name for themselves as a team to watch, the Cubs were not yet ready to play big schools like Paducah Tilghman. Because the Cubs were not only good basketball players but good imitators of the Harlem Globetrotters, folks from all around the county came to see them play. At that time the second or B team (called the junior varsity now) played before the varsity played. When the word got out that Coach Story's B team was better than his varsity, people came to watch and root for the B team, and they skipped attending the varsity games. Important to note, too, is that no other team had done what Cuba did: announce publicly its goal of winning the state championship. Its mission statement, the first of its kind for Cuba, at least, was adopted by the entire tenth-grade class. Before long the whole little high school adopted it and carried the idea out into the community. People weren't accustomed to hearing kids say that they had a goal in mind and were working toward achieving it. Instead of saying "if," the Cuba folks began saying, "When Cuba wins that championship, won't that be a grand day!"

The Cubs loved being the topic of conversation at the store and in the churchyards. Someone would ask, "Say, did you notice how much Doodle has grown over the summer? He should tear them up this year. And how 'bout Howie! He's running faster than a deer. Why, nobody will be able to take the ball away from him!" Folks would talk for hours about the boys, recalling things they had seen the pair do when they were small. They would even argue about who would make the starting five and wonder how the boys were going to be able to play and get their chores done at the same time.

By late summer 1949, Doodle and Howie wanted nothing to do with farm work and had decided that if they worked harder at their basketball they could go to the state tournament the next year instead of waiting for their senior year. When Willie sent Howie out to top their two-acre patch of tobacco, Doodle went along to help. Topping tobacco is a tedious, time-consuming task that requires cutting the top off every single tobacco plant, except the few you want

120

to let flower to collect seeds from later. Topping tobacco prevents the plant from flowering and helps it leaf out broadly and nicely.

The boys despised working with tobacco and to ease their job they took a basketball to the field with them. Instead of topping the tobacco in a neat uniform manner, they ran down the rows, each topping two rows at a time in an attempt to get the work finished quickly. At the end of the rows, they'd practice their ball-handling, then they'd turn and go back, topping two more rows each. When they were done, the field had, as one observer explained, "an uneven, zig-zaggy look," with some rows of plants much taller than the others. It was, as the store setters exclaimed, a disgraceful-looking patch, looking like "a dern drunk had topped it!" Old Willie Crittenden was burnt up about it, too, and took a lot of teasing from the store setters all that summer and fall.

For Christmas 1949, W. A. mailed Howie a basketball, the finest he could buy. It was the first real basketball Howie ever owned. After having played with old rag-filled balls for so long at home, he was thrilled. That Christmas morning, sleet was coming down in sheets. Four inches of snow already covered the ground. It was impossible to work or to play outside. Howie hugged the new ball, spun it around on his finger, pitched it up in the air several times. Then he began quietly throwing it over the opened door between the kitchen and living room and catching it when it bounced off the floor. Willie, in his rocking chair in the living room, watched silently a few seconds. Then he jumped out of his chair, angrily snatched the ball from the boy's hand, and limped into the kitchen as Howie protested. Willie flung the back door open and threw the ball as far as he could out into the yard and ordered Howie to sit and be quiet. Howie's eyes filled with tears. Fearful that the ball might freeze and be ruined if he didn't go get it immediately, he begged his father to let him get it. Willie returned to his rocking chair, refusing to look at the boy and saying, "Gonna teach you a lesson, boy."

With hot tears streaming down his face, Howie looked at his mother, who stood leaning against the kitchen window, staring at

121

the ball as it gradually disappeared behind the film of sleet. Willie closed his eyes as if to nap. Silently, Alta Ruth wrapped her woolen shawl around her head and shoulders, slipped out the back door, and picked up the basketball. She ran back into the house and handed it to Howie, who stood in the doorway with Helen watching. No word passed between the mother and son. With the cold basketball pressed between them, they hugged each other tightly with tears glistening on their faces. Howie hid the ball under his bed and never played with it in the house again.

That summer of 1949, the state highway department blacktopped the gravel road that ran from Mayfield to Cuba to Pilot Oak. Howie and Doodle were ecstatic. They finally had a hard surface on which to play ball when they couldn't play in the gym in Cuba. In the stillness of many hazy summer afternoons, villagers could hear that basketball pounding on the pavement. When the moon was full, they played late into the night in all kinds of weather. This year-round outdoor competition, even in the deepest of winter, primed them for playing in all conditions.

By the time the Cubs were sophomores, they were good and they knew it. Basketball had become the most important thing in their lives, and that's exactly what Coach Story wanted to happen. Just about the time the season got started, Old "Bear" Wiggins, a well-known "bird-dog" (someone who tattles on everyone else) told Coach Story that he saw Joe Buddy smoking a cigarette in front of Wagoner's. Coach Story never laid down rules about what the boys were to eat, when to go to bed, or who to date, but he did forbid smoking cigarettes. Oddly enough, he never complained if they chewed tobacco and even provided spit cans, which he had stationed around the gym floor. Except for Howie, all of them chewed tobacco and occasionally smoked cigars and cigarettes, too. They chewed Days Work or twist tobacco that the local farmers twisted themselves. The day he confronted Joe Buddy, Coach Story stared at the boy through narrow slits of eyes, and told him, "You can't smoke and play basketball. Smoking cuts your wind off and keeps you from running. Cain't use

Joe Buddy Warren was a key supporting player for the Cubs, although he was not exempt from Coach Story's discipline when word got back to the coach that Joe Buddy had been seen smoking a cigarette. (Photo courtesy of Jimmie Webb)

you! Won't use you! You're suspended for three weeks from practice. Meanwhile, you can think about what you want to do." Lost in astonishment, Joe Buddy was dumbstruck. He figured he was too important to the team to get suspended and wondered how the coach would get along without him. But he soon learned that the coach got along fine.

Joe's pal Ted got into trouble, too, and Coach Story taught him a lesson. In a game with Kirksey, during the third quarter Ted, for some unknown reason, was standing under the goalpost by himself—snowbirding, as it is called. Except for the opposing player who

123

was a foot taller than Ted, no one else was near him. One of the Cubs threw the ball the length of the court to Ted, who caught it, looked over his shoulder, and saw his opponent standing there. With his back to the goalpost, Ted threw the ball backward over his head and missed the basket. Coach Story pulled him out immediately. The next day, at practice, he called Ted over to a side goalpost, tossed him a ball, saying curtly, "Shoot the ball." Ted shot it. "Shoot it again," said Coach Story, "and keep shooting it until I come back." He turned and walked away. About an hour later, he returned. He asked Ted, "Have you missed any baskets?" Ted replied, "Yes, sir." Coach Story said, "Well, just keep shooting until I come back."

Ted got so tired he could hardly lift the ball, but he was afraid to stop shooting for fear that Coach Story was watching him from some place in the gym. Finally, at three o'clock, when it was time to board the buses for home, Coach Story appeared and asked him, "Have you missed any more baskets?" Ted answered, "Yes, sir, I have." Coach Story told him, "The lesson I am teaching you is this: When you get to the point where you cannot miss a shot when you're looking at the basket, *then* you can shoot over your head without looking at it."

Coach Story got after Raymon for letting a player dribble around him. "You let a guy dribble around you, you can head for the bench. Cause that's where you gonna stay."

During practices and even during games, Jimmie Webb, who was lovesick, would always be looking around for Martha Layne Casey, instead of paying attention to instructions. He was a talented ballplayer, a high scorer, but was easily distracted. Coach Story would get angry, but he would never fuss at him the way he fussed at the others, probably because Jimmie had an endearing, almost naive quality that made him a hard kid to get mad at. At one of the games, Coach Story told him: "Jimmie, I want you to get under the basket and then come back out and get in the corner. We'll try to get the ball to you so you can shoot a jump shot from there. Do you understand what you're to do?" No, Jimmie did not. While the instructions were being given, he was daydreaming,

Jimmie Webb could score a lot of points on
the basketball court, although there would be
times he would be so distracted looking
around for Martha during practices or time-
outs that he would miss out on some of the
coach's instructions. (Photo courtesy of
Donald Poyner)

looking up in the stands for Martha. Surprising everyone there that
time, Coach Story lost his temper. He closed his fist and banged it
up and down under Jimmie's chin several times really hard, making
the boy's teeth slam together, and his head hurt so bad he saw
flashing lights. From then on, Coach Story had the boy's attention.

*   *   *

Jimmie's dad had an old 1930 Ford Model A coupe with a rumble
seat. It was not licensed. It had no windshield, no brakes, and no

125

lights. And the only way the doors could be opened was from the outside. The shift had three forward gears and a reverse, but it would not stay in gear. Unless the driver held it in the gear he wanted, it always popped back into neutral. So Jimmie learned to drive the old car by holding the gearstick in one hand and the steering wheel in the other. Although he did not have a driver's license, he was allowed to drive the car as long as he stayed close to home and on the local roads. He soon abused this privilege and drove the old heap all over the county day and night. Friends riding with him at night used to hang out the windows holding flashlights so he could see where he was driving. One night, while he was out with his friends Ted Bradley, Leon Brann, Donald Wray, Don Payne, and Mason Harris, they decided to go to Mayfield—a big mistake. The north side of the courthouse in downtown Mayfield is uphill. As they were traveling uphill on the courthouse square, in the midst of much merriment, they were singing at the top of their voices:

Irene, Goodnight, Irene, Goodnight,
Goodnight, Irene, Goodnight, Irene, I'll see you in my dreams.
Sometimes I live in the country.
Sometimes I live in the town.
Sometimes I have a great notion to jump into the river and drown.
Irene, Goodnight, Irene, Goodnight. I'll see you in my dreams.

Just as they got to the top of a hill, the motor died. They started coasting backward. Jimmie had no brakes and couldn't put the car in gear to stop it. It rolled backward all the way down the hill and through a red light. A police car followed them for a while until Jimmie finally got the car stopped. Lacking a driver's license, Jimmie scrambled to switch places with Leon Brann, who did have one. The policeman saw that the boys were scared to death and gave them a stern warning: "No lights! Hmmm. No brakes! Hmmmm. No license. Hmmmm. No more driving. Understand?" The policeman added, "Now, you get this damned thing out of town, and I don't want to ever see it in Mayfield again."

CHAPTER 17

STANDING ROOM ONLY

"WHEN PRIDE COMES, DISGRACE COMES, BUT WITH THE HUMBLE IS WISDOM."
—PROVERBS 11:2

Cuba—1950–1951. When the school year started in the fall of 1950, the changes in all of the Cubs were noticeable. Now juniors, they had grown taller and stronger. Howie had reached his full height of six feet and was an exceptional ball handler and remarkably fast. He had few equals in passing and defense, none in dribbling. Doodle, at six-foot-four and an inch taller when he had good posture, was as limber as a rubber band. He had developed an amazing hook shot that he released with a distinctive windmill motion of his arm. He'd bring the ball from way back to directly over his head, and with his arm extended up, nobody could get to that ball. He had complete control. His shot was a high arcing one that was accurate from surprising ranges.

Six-foot-one Jimmie Webb was a rugged rebounder who liked patrolling the boards. Jimmie could score and from a long distance, too. The big burly Raymon guarded the boards like a pit bull. He was a reliable role player on the team. He had good hands, he could hold on to a ball, and he could score when needed. Raymon was physically strong, and without his defense and rebounding, the team would not have been as successful as it was. So in 1950, when

Raymon began having ankle problems, Coach Story worriedly started looking around for a backup. He found one in Bill Pollock, who played basketball for Fancy Farm, a Catholic neighborhood less than ten miles northeast of Mayfield.

A six-foot-two, dark-haired, handsome boy, Bill lived in Dublin, a neighborhood near Fancy Farm. Although Coach Story did not usually recruit players, he did negotiate through Bill's mother's cousin, who lived in Cuba. When his relative approached Bill about transferring to the Cuba school to play basketball, Bill did not object. As the only Protestant boy at the Catholic Fancy Farm, he did not have close ties to the school. Although he continued to live at home in Dublin, he transferred as a junior to Cuba. According to the rules, he was not allowed to play ball for a year after transferring. Therefore, he was made a manager so that he could travel with the Cubs. Although he practiced daily with the team, he did not play in any games in the 1950–51 season. Bill turned out to be a valuable sixth man who filled in for Raymon and for Doodle. He would have had a much bigger role in the team's effort if Coach Story had allowed him to play more. Bill was always considered an outsider, and he knew about Coach Story's preference for using the hometown boys first. Coach Story liked to work with six players: Howie, Doodle, Jimmie Webb, Joe Buddy, Raymon, and Jimmy Jones.

Joe Buddy was barely six feet tall, but he had great speed and ball-handling ability. He was a scrappy fighter who could jump and score. The only senior in the group was Jimmy Jones, a strong and dependable leader and the one who did most of the brain work on the floor. Ted Bradley was often first off the bench to replace Joe Buddy. Paul Simpson, Harold Roberts, and Jimmy Brown also were valuable reserves. Those were the boys that made up Cuba's team in 1951. Coach Story's young son Rex was the team's mascot, and the managers were Bobby McClain, Robert Peters, and Donald Poyner.

The Cubs' antics on the hardwood were the leading topic of conversation in Graves County. Not just at Harper's, Rhodes's, and Wagoner's, but at all the other stores. Discussions about crops, politics, illnesses, and deaths were replaced with what Jack Story's team was doing. Their games were so popular that crowds packed the gyms. Some home games were moved to other locations, like Mayfield and Sedalia, which had larger gyms, but the majority were played at the Cuba school.

When you entered the one-story brick school, Coach Story's office was to the left and a small storage room used for a box office was to the right. The lobby led into a long horizontal hall, with classrooms on either side and an entrance into the gym in the center. On the front left-hand side of the gym was a large round coal stove that heated the gym in the winter. The only set of bleachers, eight rows high, was also on the left side, starting near the stove. On the opposite side of the gym was a space about three feet wide that separated the inbounds line from the wall, although during ball games folding chairs were set up in this narrow lane.

As the Cuba team became more famous and a large number of fans had to be turned away for lack of space in the gym, a balcony was built above the bleachers adding three more rows of seats. Folding chairs were placed on the stage at the end of the gym's playing floor. With these additional seating arrangements, the Cuba gym could seat 450, but as many as 500 to 550 crowded in. Even then, many others were turned away. The standing crowd was so thick it rounded off the corners of the court. The court was ten or so feet short of official length anyway, and with fans standing practically on the playing floor, the Cubs got used to playing in crowded and smoky conditions. There were no laws prohibiting smoking back then.

The games started at 7:00 P.M., but people would start lining up outside the school by five. Coach Story usually arrived around six to open the doors. About that same time Em Boyd Poyner, Donald's dad and Cuba's official ticket agent, would come directly from his work at the Mayfield Merit Clothing Company without even stopping to eat supper. Em Boyd was never paid for handling ticket sales; he did it as community service as long as Coach Story was there. Rupert Bivins, another one of the Cubs' strong

Even as a toddler, Donald Poyner was seeing eye to eye with his dad
E. B. Poyner, who went on to become Cuba's official basketball ticket agent
for spectators flocking to the Cubs' games. Donald became class president and
valedictorian. He tutored a number of the players in their schoolwork. (Photo
courtesy of Donald Poyner)

supporters, took great pride in always being the first person in line
to buy a ticket.

Joe Buddy's father never missed a game or even a practice; in
fact, the joke around Cuba was that Jess had a better attendance
record than Joe Buddy did. None of the other Cubs' fathers attended any of the games until the Cubs' senior year. Then Raymon's dad started going regularly. With all the hoopla surrounding
the players, especially Doodle, Howie, and Jimmie Webb, you'd
think that their parents would have been so proud of their sons
that they'd be first in line for admission. But that was not the
case. One night when the Cubs were playing Lowes, Doodle was

surprised at halftime when someone shouted, "Hey, Doodle, your pa's here!" Vodie and two men were riding home from Mayfield where they had part-time jobs, and Vodie said the other guys wanted to stop to see how the ball game was turning out. They stayed only a few minutes, long enough for Vodie to hear his son praised and to wave hello to him.

Girls began to swoon and swoop around the ballplayers, so much so that the boys' temptation to swagger was strong. At times their success with basketball and with girls made them more than a little heady. Noticing how their manly reserve had vanished, Coach Story warned them about what happened to teams that got the big head. But they did not listen.

When the 1949–1950 Cubs advanced to the regionals at Murray State University, they played the opening round against Cayce. Two weeks earlier, the Cubs had thoroughly whipped Cayce, 92-36, in Cayce's gym. Doodle scored fifty-two points. When the regional game came up, the Cubs were overly confident. They had just gotten new uniforms and, for the first time, had warm-ups. They had no doubts about their going to the state tournament and were enthusiastic and eager to go. But a day or so before the game was to be played on March 9, 1950, Coach Story learned that two of Cuba's starters, Don Stone, a senior, and Raymon McClure, a sophomore, would be unable to play in this opening round. Raymon had the mumps and Don had injured his knee. Although Coach Story was concerned about losing these two players, the other Cubs were not. In fact, Doodle boasted that he and Howie alone, with one hand tied behind them, could lick little Cayce.

As the high scorer, Doodle felt immensely superior to Cayce. He thought playing Cayce was a waste of time. Before the game started, he provided the entertainment for the crowd. As he strutted before the bleachers, chewing on an unlit cigar, he boasted to the crowd about how Cuba was going to whip "poor little Cayce." He'd point toward the Cayce players and say such things as "Why, I wouldn't play with that outfit!" He'd yell to them: "Aren't y'all scared? Well, y'all oughta be. Y'all gonna play Cuba tonight!

Y'all remember what Cuba did to you before, don't you?" He even criticized their uniforms. At one point, he lifted his long hairy leg, flaunting his new shoes, and said, "Do y'all see these? Y'all never seen shoes like these! Have y'all? Now look at your poor old shoes. Why, we got better uniforms, better everything than what you've got! Y'all gonna cry? Go ahead and cry now." The crowd, roaring with laughter, encouraged him to go on. He sauntered up and down, before the spectators, telling Cayce how mighty powerful the Cuba Cubs were and how badly Cuba was going to beat them. He shouted, "Y'all look scared. Y'all look like a long-tail cat in a room full of rocking chairs." Everyone loved his silly banter and laughed; everyone, except Coach Story. He was angry. The veins in his neck and forehead stood out and his eyes looked black because his pupils were so dilated. Of course, Doodle was having such a good time that he never glanced at the coach. If he had, he would have been less mouthy.

Doodle entered the Cayce game as if it were some kind of joke. During the entire first half, he goofed off, letting Cayce score, thinking that he and his buddies could turn up the heat and burn Cayce out anytime they got ready. Every so often in the first half, Doodle would put his hand to his ear, cock his head to the side, and call out to the spectators, "Who's ahead?" Someone would shout back, "Cayce!" and the audience would laugh. The Cuba partisans found his act amusing, too, knowing that the Cubs could run their score up on Cayce whenever they got ready. At the end of the first half, as he was going down to the dressing room, Doodle yelled again, "Who's ahead?" The crowd laughingly shouted "Cayce! Cayce—42-37!" Everyone that night was having a great time.

The second half started. Cayce scored again, but the Cubs were having too much fun to go into action. But when they got ready to score, they couldn't. Before they realized it, the clock ran out and the final answer to "Who's ahead?" was "Cayce!" Doodle couldn't believe it. Cayce, of all teams, had given Cuba a shellacking that Cuba would never forget. Stunned, embarrassed, and full of self-doubt, Doodle and the others left the floor dejectedly. When the game was replayed on the radio the next day, he listened because he still could not believe Cuba had lost to Cayce, of all teams, and lost because of his foolishness. He had disgraced himself, his team, and his coach. Doodle scored only four points that night. Jack Story never said a word to Doodle or to any of the others. He believed in letting them learn some things the hard way.

In their years of playing together, the Cubs never had a lower moment or a more humbling experience than that Cayce game. It haunted them a long time. It taught them that anybody, as Coach Story had often told them, could beat them at a given time, that they always had to be awake to that fact. They entered their junior year subdued and matured with the weight of their expectations upon them. They weren't promising underclassmen anymore. They were the varsity—the Cuba Cubs.

*   *   *

For teenagers, there was nothing much to do in Cuba—no drive-ins, no places for them to hang out, except the stores. The Cubs often got restless before basketball season started and invented mischief. On Halloween 1950, Ted, Jimmy Jones, Paul Simpson, Howie, Joe Buddy, and Doodle decided to play a prank on some younger boys, who were three or four grades behind them. These younger boys always wanted to be around the players, pestering them, and were getting to be a nuisance. Around dusk, the older boys eased down to Joe McPherson's house and told Joe they were going to play a trick on some kids and needed his help. "We're gonna act like we are going to turn over your outhouse. We want you to see us and yell at us. Then fire this shotgun, pretending to hit one of us." Joe Buddy had taken the shell out of his shotgun, poured the lead out, crimped up the edges of the blank, and stuck the shell back into the barrel. He handed the shotgun to Joe, who agreed to participate. Just before it got dark, they rounded up the smaller boys, inviting them to join their fun for the evening. They all ran to McPherson's backyard and starting pushing over the outhouse.

133

By the time he was a sophomore, Doodle was already able to palm a basketball. (Photo courtesy of Charles Floyd)

As planned, McPherson stepped out on his porch and yelled angrily, "Hey, what y'all doing?" The big boys feigned fear, which struck terror in the younger ones. As they all started running away, Joe fired the shotgun. They could feel and smell the gun powder whizzing around them. Jimmy Jones screamed and fell down, pretending he had been shot. The smaller boys, terrified at seeing Jimmy lying facedown on the ground, went berserk. One ran crying right through a pond; another ran into a barbed-wire fence. But little Bobby Johnson ran to Harper's for help. Pauline Harper, the store owner, and the others in the store did not know what had happened when the child burst into the store talking loudly and frantically. As he stood trembling, gasping for breath, trying to explain what he had just seen, he peed in his pants standing right there in the store. "My goodness! What's wrong, Bobby?" cried Pauline as she observed the puddle under his bare feet. The little boy answered shakily, "Joe McPherson—that old sonabitch—has shot Jimmy Jones dead!" A racket outside interrupted him. When Pauline looked out the window and saw Doodle, Joe Buddy, and Ted looking in laughing, she too broke out in laughter.

CHAPTER 18

SKULL SESSIONS

"EDUCATION HAS FOR ITS OBJECT, THE FORMATION OF CHARACTER."
—HERBERT SPENCER

Cuba, Kentucky—1950–1951. The Cubs opened the 1950–51 season with big wins over Lowes, 81-48, and Cayce, 75-36. As juniors with an enviable reputation, they were preening like rock stars the night they were scheduled to play at Lynn Grove, a nearby small, poorly built rural school. Although they had never forgotten their mistake in the Cayce game the year before, they did not see any harm in having a little fun with Lynn Grove.

For days before the game, the southern end of the county had been hit with a torrential downpour. The day of the game, rain poured steadily in opaque sheets. The gym at Lynn Grove had been built on ground level without a foundation. In hard rains, the water seeped through the gym floor and washed across it. Knowing the conditions of the gym and thinking that they were far more sophisticated than their competition, Howie, Doodle, Joe Buddy, Ted, and Jimmie Webb decided to dress for the occasion. They never had practice on game days, just "skull sessions" where Coach Story would talk to them about plays. As soon as Coach Story dismissed them that afternoon, they changed clothes. They put on bib overalls, straw hats, and green rubber hip boots (the ones they wore when coon hunting). With black shoe polish, they painted "Cuba" all over the hip boots. Outfitted to mock their opponents,

136

they piled into an old 1936 Model A Ford that Doodle had borrowed from his brother Bill. The car had a '38 transmission, a '42 motor, and mechanical brakes that had been changed to hydraulic ones. The original bucket seats had been replaced with seats from an old couch. The front of the car was all exposed; it didn't have a hood. The muffler had gone out, and Bill had taken a weld pipe and bent it to meet the curvature of the axle. That way, those riding in the car couldn't really hear the awful noise it was making, but people for miles around could hear it.

As they were driving along that country road making a tremendous racket, they were happy and confident and eager to meet the world. There was no doubt in their minds that they could conquer the world. Unable to resist any opportunity to show off, they stopped at the Lynn Grove store to buy pops. Doodle immediately became the center of attention. Chewing on his unlit cigar, he strutted around, greeting all the store setters and complimenting one of the old guys who was dressed in brand-new denim overalls and red plaid shirt. "Why, sir," he said, "you look like a third-Monday mule!" They all laughed. Back then, that remark was a genial expression said to a person dressed nicely. It stemmed from the time when farmers went to Trade Day in Mayfield on the third Monday in March. Before some of them traded their old mules, they did some cosmetic work on the mule's teeth. Usually, a good mule trader can tell what age a mule is by examining his teeth, but not always. It's as hard to tell a mule's age sometimes as it is to tell a pretty woman's age. Some mule men were experts at fixing an old mule's teeth to make him appear younger than he was and they earned good money doing it. So an old mule that had been allowed to rest a few days and had gotten his teeth fixed would look pretty darn good, except maybe to a real mule trader. Hence, the expression, "You look like a third-Monday mule!"

The mood in the store darkened when Doodle insulted the store loafers with his first question: "Do any of y'all play basketball around here?" The response evoked a lively discussion that went on for nearly half an hour.

137

When they arrived at the school, Coach Story was standing by the coal stove in one corner of the gym talking to the other coach. When he saw his boys in those outfits, his mood got as dark as his suit. But he did not say a word except, "Hurry up and get dressed."

The Lynn Grove team was not good at all. The Cubs should have beaten them by forty points at least, but the final score was 63-40 because the Cubs thought they were a whole lot better than they were. Coach Story was so angry by the end of the third quarter that he ordered Howie, Doodle, Joe Buddy, and Jimmie Webb out of the game and told them to get dressed. They sat on the bench, scrunched down, with shame, as they watched Raymon, Bill, Paul, Jimmy Jones, and Jimmy Brown finish the last quarter.

After Lynn Grove, they defeated Melber, 93-42; Fancy Farm, 59-40; and Sedalia, 71-44, making six consecutive wins. The next game was one in which the Farmington team opened up with a slow-down, a ball-control technique. Cuba got the lead and responded by holding the ball, winning the game, 22-10. Then came wins over Murray, 60-27; Symsonia, 58-35; and Fulton, 66-50, giving Cuba a perfect 10-0 start.

During the Graves County Christmas Tournament, the Cubs defeated Symsonia, 47-38; Wingo, 74-50; and Sedalia, 66-39. From there they went to the Paducah Christmas Tournament, a prestigious competition. In the opening round, the Cubs defeated Hardin, 52-40, for their fourteenth consecutive win of the season. Then in the tournament's second game, their sixth game in a week, Cuba played what was to be their worst game of the entire season; they lost to Cave-in-Rock, 58-36. This outstanding team from Illinois stunned Cuba by using the full-court zone press, a tactic that surprised Coach Story and the Cubs, who were not prepared for this defense. Howie would get the ball and throw it behind his back to change his dribble and a Cave-in-Rock guy would come up behind Howie's back on Howie's blind side, get the ball, and lay it in. All five of the Cave-in-Rock crew were incredibly fast, and they were all over the court, baffling the disorganized Cuba. Players later said this was the only time that they ever saw Coach Story outcoached and unable to respond to another team's tactics.

The full-court zone press was not the only thing that confused the Cubs on that trip. The night before they played Cave-in-Rock, several of them, without Coach Story's knowledge, walked all over one end of Paducah, looking for 808 Washington Street, where, they had been told, there was a whorehouse. They knew nothing about whorehouses and not much about women or sex, but they were curious. They knew nothing about Paducah either, and must have walked ten miles searching for the place. After they finally found their destination, they nervously entered the establishment and were shocked to learn the fee for the services. They excused themselves politely and stepped outside, whispering anxiously about what they were to do. At one point they even considered running back to the motel. After they pooled all their money, they counted out only five dollars—the price of one admission. Since all of them could not go back into the house, they decided to let one go. Slapping the money into the hands of the shiest virgin in the group, they shoved him up the steps, pushed him through the door, and closed it behind him. That night's activity was one that Coach Story never learned about.

Back into the regular-season play, the Cubs won over Brewers, 80-41; Murray, 90-40; Wingo, 97-65; and Nortonville, 43-35. Next they rolled over Mayfield, 71-31; and took the Lowes Blue Devils, 86-48. At that point, Cuba had twenty wins and one loss for the 1950–51 season.

Playing this number of games took them away from the classroom days at a time. They could not possibly keep up with their classwork and did not even try. By that time the starters, especially, were so protected by Coach Story that the tutors were superfluous. The teachers got the most work they could out of the players whenever they were in class and then turned their heads. Most of the players continued to make grades good enough to stay eligible because the teachers simply did not expect them to do as much as the other students and gave them grades on whatever they did.

No one believed that this behavior was right, but everyone—teachers included—was caught in the hype of the time. Cuba had never been special before, and these boys were making Cuba special. The whole community supported the team. No one questioned anything that Coach Story did. The basketball players had gotten to the point where they knew they were special, not only to the community and to the pretty girls who flocked around them, but also to their coach. Most of the teachers, accepting the situation, ignored the boys' absences. In turn, the players ignored the few teachers who tried to maintain academic standards.

Doodle, Joe Buddy, and Ted were more mischievous than the other boys. Thinking of themselves as comedians with obligations to entertain the other students, they were notorious for disturbing class. At one point they started wearing flat-top hats, a style popular then. They'd take men's old hats and beat them down flat and plunk them on their heads in a rakish manner as they sauntered about the schoolyard. Although they did not wear the hats inside the building, they'd take them into class and fool with them, annoying the teachers. One morning in typing class, Joe Buddy and Ted started misbehaving every time the teacher turned her back to write on the board. At one point in the lesson, Joe turned to Ted and boldly asked aloud, "Is it snowing?" Ted answered he didn't know but that he'd find out. Interrupting the lesson, Ted rose from his desk and walked over to the window and said, "Yep, it's snowing." Frustrated and inexperienced, the young teacher, a pretty woman who was new to Cuba, got angry and ordered him and Joe Buddy to leave the room immediately and go to the principal's office. The two of them smiled arrogantly, put their hats on their heads, and strolled out as the whole class broke down laughing.

When Coach Story, whom they met in the hall, asked, "What's the problem?" Ted and Joe said, "Well, sir, she kicked us out. We didn't do anything. We don't know what we did that upset her. Mr. Story, you know how some women are." He asked, "What do you mean?" Joe told him, "Well, sir, she was just in a bad mood or something. I know that we did not do anything." Coach Story stared at them hard for a few seconds as they tried to maintain their posture. Then he led them back to the class, where he told the typing students to go to study hall and asked the teacher to meet with him in his office. No one but Coach Story and the teacher knew what transpired between them that morning, but before school was out that afternoon, the teacher tearfully apologized to Joe and Ted. As soon as the semester ended, she resigned and moved away. Certainly, Coach Story's behavior in this case is impossible to explain or defend.

Until the consolidation of the schools in the 1940s, Dr. Marion Page, the physician for southern Graves County, was the trustee for the Cuba school. Born and reared in the Cuba area, Dr. Page knew the isolation that people in the Purchase experienced and wanted to give the children opportunities to expose them to the outside world. He saw to it that the school purchased good books and maps. He sponsored talent shows regularly for the students and the community. He even performed in some of them himself. During the 1930s, he bought movies (some were old silent films) and showed them via a creaky film projector in the auditorium on Friday nights.

As the trustee whose job it was to hire all the teachers and principals, Dr. Page insisted that the faculty come from places other than Graves County and the Purchase, if at all possible. He wanted not only his own four children, but all the children in Cuba, to be exposed to ideas, beliefs, and cultures other than their own. While he was trustee, he provided room and board in his own home for the new single teachers. He believed that the more his own children were in the company of educated people, on a personal and academic level, the more likely they were to grow intellectually and to learn how to be tolerant of different views. At the evening meals in the Page home, the teachers and family shared interesting conversations, but they seldom discussed sports.

After he retired as trustee, the new superintendent and board of education did not hold Dr. Page's views. More local people were given teaching positions. Perhaps for that reason among many

141

others, academic standards may have been less effectively upheld. Although it is clear that he expected all the students to do their best and to behave, Jack Story put far more emphasis on basketball than he did on academics. The group of boys he was coaching at this particular time had such extraordinary ability and such an extraordinary chance to excel in basketball that he did not want to sacrifice the opportunity. He knew, too, that his players would never go to college unless they had athletic scholarships. They probably would not have even graduated from high school had they not been involved in basketball. In those days, the incentive of being successful in sports was a surefire way of getting boys to graduate from high school. Coach Story must have figured that if he could get them into a college, they would go on through and eventually build better lives for themselves. Without a college education, their lives would be not much different from those of their parents.

Just as their parents had done, many of the teenagers married before they graduated from high school. After the 1950 fall semester had begun, Raymon married a young girl from Mayfield.

Raymon McClure joined Jimmie Webb as Cubs players who were married during their days at Cuba. (Photo courtesy of Donald Poyner)

Jimmie Webb and Martha Layne Casey married at Martha's parents' home on Saturday, September 29, 1951, at the beginning of their senior year. Drennan Bagwell was best man and Carolyn Work, maid of honor. Carolyn cried before the ceremony, all through the ceremony, and afterward. Those attending the wedding thought she was crying because her best friend was getting married. But that was not the case. The day before the ceremony, Carolyn had learned that she was not elected cheerleader. She was so upset she started crying and didn't stop crying until three days later. Dorothy Williams, Martha's sister, and her husband, L. T., took the family, the wedding guests, and the newlyweds to Sue and Charlie's Cafe at Kentucky Lake for a fish supper. Afterward, Jimmie and Martha, in Jimmie's uncle's 1948 Ford, left for their honeymoon at Ervin's Motel in Mayfield.

A PILGRIMAGE

Early in January 1951, the Cubs lost their second game of the season when Clark County, the number-one team in the state rankings, beat them, 62-61. The day the Cubs left for Winchester to play Clark County, snow was falling so thick in Kentucky you couldn't see your hand in front of you. They left early that morning because Winchester was twenty miles on the other side of Lexington, an eight-hour drive. For out-of-town games most of the starters rode with Coach Story, and the other players went with Joe McPherson. Jess Warren seldom drove his car out of Graves County; but for some reason that morning, Jess was driving Howie, Doodle, Ted, and Joe Buddy to Winchester. The highways were dangerously slick with ice, and as darkness began to fall, the roads got slicker.

When he got just outside of Lexington, Jess noticed a slight rise in the highway and a highway sign which he couldn't see to read. Thinking that he was about to approach a hill, he figured he'd better speed up because he didn't want to get halfway up an icy hill and not have enough power to get over it. So he floorboarded the gas pedal and had sped ahead about thirty yards when they all abruptly realized that they were going downhill and at a breakneck speed. Much to their horror, they were headed toward the narrow ice-covered bridge spanning the deep Kentucky River. Holding on to the steering wheel tightly, trying to control the car, Jess bit the stem off his pipe as his car skimmed and skidded over the frozen road and rolled onto the bridge at great speed. No one said a word until they crossed that bridge and then they all sighed with relief. By the time they arrived in Winchester, they were tired, cold, and shaken.

The Clark County game was followed by a win over Farmington, 76-45. Completely outclassed, Farmington decided to hold the ball on Cuba and for a while Cuba went along with them but led, 18-8, at the half. During the break the Cubs told Coach Story they were bored with the slow game and asked if they could put on their Globetrotters act, something that they had not done thus far in any game. Figuring the fans would enjoy the performance more than the stall, he said it was all right with him.

As the Cubs went into their act, doing all the tricks they had seen the Globetrotters do, the crowd went wild. Doodle transformed himself into the nimble, ageless Goose Tatum. Howie turned into Marques Haynes, the great dribbler. Jimmie Webb became Ermar Robertson, the set-shot artist, and Raymon, the agile Billy Brown. The only Cub who played himself was Jimmy Jones. Propelled by the crowd's enthusiasm and excitement, the Cubs played baseball and even attempted a football field goal while poor Farmington looked aghast and helpless. When the game was over, the crowd gave the Cubs a standing ovation.

Their performance that night established their reputation as the "most colorful high school team ever to play basketball." The Associated Press picked up the story about that game and an article about the Cuba Cubs appeared in newspapers across the nation. Within a few days after the article appeared, Coach Story got a call from Abe Saperstein, the manager of the Harlem Globetrotters, inviting him and the Cubs to come to Saint Louis as his guests for an appearance with the Globetrotters. That trip was one of the highlights of their lives. In publicity for the Trotters' Saint Louis visit, Saperstein capitalized on the opportunity by inserting in the programs photographs of Doodle with Tatum, Howie with Haynes, Coach Story with Saperstein.

A rumor that persisted for years claimed that Jack Story's success was accidental, that Story had no coaching experience and had written to Adolph Rupp asking to borrow one of his films. Rupp, it was said, accidentally sent him a Globetrotters film, so Story's Cuba Cubs were just plain lucky. That rumor bothered Story because it was so blatantly false.

After the spectacular event with Farmington, the Cubs beat Fulton, 70-40, and Wingo, 90-63. In the annual Mayfield Charities Invitational Game, they beat the highly ranked Lone Oak's Purple Flash, 80-69. Then came victories over Symsonia, 77-49; Lynn Grove, 64-55; and Cayce, 92-40, to end the 1950-51 regular season with twenty-seven wins and two losses.

Cuba then embarked on a commanding march through the district tournament and into the regionals. They opened the district tournament with an 86-45 defeat of Lowes. In the semifinals, they took Sedalia, 62-51, and then Mayfield, 74-29, in the finals to win the district championship, extending their record to 30-2.

In the 1951 regional tournament, Cuba met Paducah Tilghman, the defending regional champion. Tilghman was tall and strong, with players destined for All-American collegiate careers in football and basketball. The game was memorably rough. As fascinated as the crowd was with Howie's dazzling dribbling and Doodle's hook shot, Tilghman was determined not to lose. Its players used some rough tactics in guarding Cuba. Instead of their hands, they used their fingernails in grabbing for the ball, and they dug into Cuba flesh every chance they got.

Cuba built a lead and in the second half played a deliberate game, holding the ball for prolonged periods. The Cubs took only fifteen shots in the entire half and hit eight of them. Howie provided a fancy dribbling performance that left the crowd and the Paducah team gasping. Jimmy Jones scored five points in the final three minutes of play. Tilghman players went from frustration to desperation, literally scratching and clawing to get back into the

game. When Doodle fouled out with two minutes to go, his uniform was stained with blood. But the Cubs held on. Tilghman
pulled to within two points with twenty-three seconds to go, but
Cuba held on to win, 51-46. Coach Story congratulated his team,
saying he was proud that they did not respond in kind to Tilghman's ruthless attempts to get ahead. He repeated what he had so
often said: "You beat your opponent by outplaying him, by out-
smarting him, by being better than he is, not by cheating."

With that victory, the stage was set for Cuba to go against
Wickliffe for the regional championship. If they won this game,
they'd go to the state tournament. They faced Wickliffe eagerly and
enthusiastically knowing that they had to fight all the way because
Wickliffe, disappointed the previous year in the finals against Tilghman, was even more determined this time around. Wickliffe's
crown prince was Phil Rollins, a tremendous athlete whom the
newspapers described as the "classy cager." Called "Fantastic Phil,"
he was every bit the All-American that he had been rated in 1951.
A junior, like most of the Cubs, Rollins was a smooth worker who
rebounded on defense and sparked Wickliffe in its brilliant drive.
But even Rollins could not stop Cuba that night.

Although Wickliffe opened in the first minute and a half
with an 8-1 lead, the Cubs got to rolling like wildfire and ran
their lead to 22-12 in the first quarter. At one time in the second
period, Cuba had a fifteen-point lead before Rollins made three
baskets to trim the margin to 40-29 at halftime. Doodle was out
of the game nearly all of the third period because of personal fouls
but returned to the court in the fourth period, beefing Cuba's
score to 51-40. Wickliffe started making its dramatic comeback at
this point when Poole, Rollins, Shockly, and Morgan rocked the
Cubs as they kept coming back. The Blue Tigers never could overcome that lead, though they furiously crept up some in the fourth
quarter. But Cuba was alert in rebounding and threw up a defense
that Wickliffe could not penetrate. Jimmie Webb, Raymon, and
Howie aided Doodle in controlling both backboards. And it
was this rebounding that heaved a decisive point in the contest.

With only a minute and a half left in the game and Cuba leading at 62-59, Rollins drove in for a layup, tossed the ball, but missed. He was benched because of personal fouls, but he had played a good game. The leading scorer, he earned twenty-five points. Cuba ended up winning, 65-59.

In the scoring column for Cuba in that game, Doodle had nineteen points; Howie, eighteen; Jimmy Jones, twelve; Jimmie Webb, seven; Raymon, seven; and Joe Buddy, two. The president of Murray State College, Dr. Ralph Woods, presented the trophies that evening. Jubilant supporters mobbed the Cubs and Coach Story with affection, hugging and kissing them, lifting them onto their shoulders. At that moment, Graves County began planning a big send-off for the Cubs, who were headed for the '51 state tournament.

Cuba was the fourth Graves County school in history to make it to the state tournament. The first to go was Lowes in 1932, then Clear Spring in 1933, followed by Pilot Oak in 1937. It was Pilot Oak's trip that had inspired the twenty-year-old Jack Story to coach a state championship team.

On the day they were to leave for Lexington, Coach Story was up long before daybreak. He had been up most of the night, pacing, unable to rest. Before she fell asleep, his wife lay in bed listening to his footsteps crunching on the graveled driveway as he walked up and down in the darkness alone. Around four in the morning, he woke her gently, telling her it was time for him to leave. He kissed her good-bye, told her to be careful driving to Lexington, and said he'd see her and the kids later that afternoon. Wrapping her robe around her, she followed him to the kitchen door, where they kissed again. As she stood in the doorway watching him drive down their driveway, the moon came out from behind a cloud and shone brightly in the black sky as if to light Jack's way. She thought that was a good omen.

Joe McPherson and Jess Warren were already at Harper's waiting for him when he arrived. From there each man in his own car drove down the country roads, gathering the players, one by one, farm by farm. The early morning air smelled fresh and cold. The farmlands were wet with dew.

By the time the coach and players were well out of Mayfield on Kentucky 80, the sun was behind the clouds, making the sky the color of garnet, ruby, and emerald, and a mist stretched across the horizon like a peach satin ribbon.

The myth is that everybody in Cuba went to the state tournament that year except Harry McClain, father of team manager Bobby McClain. Harry was supposed to have stayed at home because he had a mechanical milking device rigged up on his pickup truck and could tend to everybody's cows. Harry did look after things for a lot of folks while they were in Lexington, but he was not the only person left in Cuba. What really happened was so many people from the area left that it *looked* like Graves County had been vacated.

The old school buses were in no shape to make the long trip, so everyone who had a car or truck offered to take those who did not. It was a wonderful communal effort. By 4:00 A.M. that Wednesday, March 17, 1951, the entire community was awake and bustling about. Pickups and cars were parked outside of the stores in Pilot Oak and Cuba where people were to meet to share rides. Large groups from Lynnville, Water Valley, Sedalia, Dukedom, and Fulton, plus many more from Paducah, Mayfield, Murray, and all in between gathered at the stores and at schools to form caravans and car pools. In that merry pilgrimage that morning were Cubs' supporters from Blandville, Hopkinsville, Calvert City, Madisonville, Henderson, and many other places. With the heavy traffic on Highway 31W headed north, it looked as if western Kentucky were being evacuated. Yet many stayed home, unable to go for one reason or another. Among those who stayed home were Doodle's, Howie's, and Jimmie Webb's parents.

Coach Story never put much value on cheerleaders and thought they were a major distraction for the players, at best. He made no arrangements for them, so they rode with their families or friends. Because they had not made reservations early enough, the cheerleaders could not get rooms in any of the hotels and motels in

Lexington. They ended up staying in Versailles, a few miles outside of Lexington, and that inconvenience suited Coach Story just fine.

Jimmie Webb's mother said that the folks in Graves County who didn't have radios were trying to buy them once they learned Cuba had won the regionals. In fact, all the stores in Mayfield and Fulton sold out of radios in a flash once the word was out that Coach Story was taking his crew to Lexington. The day the state tournament began, many in Pilot Oak went to Fred Wagoner's store to listen to the games on the radio there. In Cuba, the Rhodes stayed home and kept their store open so that folks could listen there. Hours before the Cubs were to play their first tournament game, Fred Rhodes had cleared out as much room as he could to make plenty of space around the radio. More than an hour before the game was to begin, folks began walking toward Rhodes's. Expectation and excitement filled the air. Because nearly every person in the area had contributed to the Cubs' effort in some way, each person felt as if he or she had a stake in the Cubs' success. The farmers had scraped together enough money to buy the boys new warm-up suits, socks, and underwear. Aught McClain, the father of the Cubs' classmate Al McClain, was a barber and gave free haircuts to Coach Story and each of the players. Mrs. Story bought the boys their new satiny gold and green uniforms with earnings she had saved from the concession stand she ran at the school. Some men who had jobs in Mayfield collected money to buy basketballs, which Coach Story had painted in the school colors—gold and green.

Mayfield had four men's clothing stores and the owners of the stores, Reece Barton, C. B. Hargrove, Joe Lookofsky, Edwin Wilson, and Watt Seay (these last two were partners) got together and gave each player and Coach Story a complete suit of clothes, including shirts, ties, socks, shoes, topcoats, and underwear. Willie Foster and other Mayfield merchants collected enough money to pay for the team's travel expenses, hotel rooms, meals, and to give each player a brand-new twenty-dollar bill, an extravagant amount of spending money in those days. Everything that could be done had been done and now the rest was up to the Cubs.

CHAPTER 20

SHOWTIME

"O WONDERFUL, WONDERFUL, AND MOST WONDERFUL WONDERFUL, AND YET
AGAIN WONDERFUL."

—SHAKESPEARE

Lexington, Kentucky—March 1951. When Coach Story parked the Kaiser in front of Memorial Coliseum that cold crisp afternoon, the doors popped open and Howie and Doodle sprang out first. Then came Joe Buddy, Raymon, Jimmie Webb, and Coach Story, dressed in a brown suit and a dark felt hat cocked to one side of his head. While the boys ran ahead, he stood for a few seconds, looking around, with his arms akimbo, hands pressing into his lower back as if to stretch and ease an old back pain. He smiled as he watched his boys bound into the brand-new coliseum, the site of the Kentucky Boys' High School Basketball Tournament.

Inside the arena, the Cubs and the coach were silently in awe. The feeling was like that of a battlefield before a battle. Then Howie broke the spell when he dropped to his knees and ran his hand over the polished blond hardwood, saying, "This floor is like glass!" Jimmie Webb looked up at the ceiling and whispered, "This is the first place I've ever been in where I know I could not throw the ball and hit the ceiling." Doodle added, "Say, Coach, you sure could haul a lotta hay in here." They all laughed and relaxed a little. This was the first time they had been so far out in the world, and they had mixed feelings of fear, wonder, and excitement. This was the moment they

151

had been dreaming about and working toward for four years. The trip from Cuba to Lexington was a long one, in more ways than one.

As Coach Story drove them to their hotel a few blocks away, they listened to the radio sports broadcaster talk about the upcoming tournament and describe them as "The Unknowns! The Underdogs! Little Cuba from way down yonder in Graves County!" They laughed nervously. Here they were only hours away from their first game with Covington Holmes, and from what that broadcaster indicated, they were not expected to survive it. The Covington Holmes team, coached by Tom Ellis, had won the Ninth Region Tournament and was considered one of the state tournament's powers—tough mentally and physically.

Twelve thousand people were packed into the coliseum that night when the teams came out for warm-ups. Peeping through the entrance waiting for their turn to run onto the court, the Cubs were as wide-eyed and jittery as a cat in a canine kennel. They had never seen so many people in one building, and they had never felt the pressure or the excitement they felt at that moment. As they looked at each other nervously, Doodle signaled for them to form a circle. Wrapping their arms around each others' shoulders, they bowed their heads silently for a moment. Then suddenly, they heard their name over the loudspeaker and the organ pumping out the strains to "Sweet Georgia Brown," the theme song of the Harlem Globetrotters and, by adoption, of the Cubs. The organist for the coliseum was Mignon Doran, wife of Adron Doran, future president of Morehead State College. Born and reared in Cuba and a graduate of the Cuba high school, Dr. Doran, along with his wife, watched with pride as the Cubs ran onto the floor bouncing basketballs painted to match their uniforms. It was showtime! And what a show the Cubs put on.

Doodle stationed himself at the free-throw line to feed balls to the other players. He did it by rolling a ball down one long arm, across his shoulders, and out the other long arm to make a pass behind his back. He'd keep the ball, fake, and dart around while spinning it on his finger and then dunk it. He'd back away and uncork

152

S H O W T I M E

his windmill shot, that high looping hook shot that he could sink from twenty feet. Suddenly, Howie erupted into an exhibition of ball handling. He darted around the court, dribbling behind his back and between his legs while running full speed. He even dribbled the ball with his butt! While moving like a dervish, he raced by Doodle, dribbling the ball between Doodle's legs. That basketball stuck with Howie as if it had been attached to his body with a magical invisible elastic band. Cage fans had never seen high school basketball players handle the ball the way these two did.

Except for those people who had watched the Cubs' warm-up routine before, the rest of the coliseum crowd had never seen such an act and weren't expecting it. In fact, they didn't know what to expect from what some were calling "this little country outfit." Although Cuba came into the tournament with the best record in the state, the team itself was a mystery. Virtually all of its games had been with teams in far western Kentucky, and even though the *Louisville Courier-Journal* picked Cuba to go as far as the semifinals, this hardly enlightened the average fan about Cuba. People weren't sure where Cuba was and weren't sure they cared. The *Courier-Journal* ran a short feature on the community.

By the end of the warm-ups, the crowd's curiosity was engaged. It's hard now to appreciate the novelty of the Cubs' style, but then it seemed a delicious heresy. The way the game was taught in those days, such brassy virtuosity was almost banned. The crowd loved it. The Covington Holmes players sneered.

During the first half, the Cubs seemed hopelessly behind. When the half ended, they trailed, 21-15. They were still trailing at the end of the third quarter, 32-27, when they suddenly sprang into action. In the first two minutes of the fourth quarter, they used an all-court press and Covington Holmes missed two shots. Joe Buddy scored on a fast break, his second basket of the game, to tie the score, 34-34. With five minutes left, Raymon made his only basket of the game to put the Cubs ahead, 36-34. With that lead, the Cubs maintained control of the ball. At that point, Howie went into his act and held the ball for most of the final six minutes

153

of the game while nearly all of the twelve thousand fans cheered with approval. Cuba beat Holmes, 38-37.

Except for the one section full of Holmes's supporters, the rest of the stadium went wild, standing and cheering for Cuba when the Cuba cheerleaders started shouting, "Two Bits! Four Bits! Six Bits a Dollar! All for Cuba, Stand Up and Holler!" Thousands of large, gas-filled, gold and green balloons were set afloat as the organist played the Cubs' theme song. The stadium was on its collective feet screaming "Cuba!" as loudly as it could.

That opening-round victory advanced the Cubs to the state quarterfinals to face the huge, highly regarded hometown team, Lexington's University High. University High had already knocked off Lexington Henry Clay, Lexington Lafayette, and Hughes Kirkpatrick—tough teams to beat—on its path to the championship and wasn't about to slow up now. Its players were rested, having had the advantage of sleeping in their own beds the night before and eating home-cooked meals. They had plenty of supporters but nothing compared to what Cuba had, for by now many of the Bluegrass locals were rooting for the little Jackson Purchase team.

Cuba took the opening tip, and Doodle, who was by now clearly a favorite with the visiting crowd, worked in for a hook shot but missed. The Purples' rebounding trio of Jimmy Flynn, Aley Harper, and Frank Tilton were living up to their sterling reputations. Flynn connected on a long set shot for the game's first points. Purples' forward Aley Harper followed with a one-hander before Doodle hooked in a shot, making it 4-2. Doodle later made a free throw, cutting University's lead to 4-3. When Flynn scored on a rebound, he was fouled by Raymon McClure. Flynn made his free throw count, putting the Purples ahead, 7-3. Joe Buddy went in to replace Raymon before forward Aley Harper made a free throw for the Purples. The Lexington club seemed to be on its way to victory after Keith Moore banked in a long shot, giving University High a confident lead, 10-3, before Cuba called time-out. University High continued to pile up points and led, 19-9, after the first quarter.

Shaken by the crowd's enthusiasm for them, the Cubs were missing most of their shots from the floor. Doodle, who had not played well in the first game, finally pulled himself together and hit three straight "Goose Tatum" hook shots. Now it was 23-18. Whenever Doodle made a hook shot, the crowd roared approval. But the alert Purples were not about to let Cuba get ahead and quickly moved back into a ten-point lead, 31-21. With three minutes left in the first half, Howie scored on a jump shot. Then Joe Buddy cashed in on a rebound just as the half ended, trimming the margin to 31-25.

In the second half, Cuba came back stronger than it had been at any time thus far in the tournament. Howie made two excellent shots; Raymon followed with another, and then Doodle powered in his jump shot, tying the score at 35-35. University High pulled out in front again, 39-36, before Doodle evened the score with only a minute and forty-five seconds to play in the quarter. Purples' forward Harper fouled out but two quick baskets kept University High ahead. Although Howie and Jimmy Jones scored, the quarter ended with University High leading, 45-43. The excited fans unabashedly clamored for the little "comeback team" Cuba to score.

Edd Kellow, sportswriter for the *Paducah Sun Democrat*, gave a firsthand description of those final minutes: "Then the roof of the entire Coliseum crumbled down on the local lads. For a west Kentucky storm, pent with the fury of a group of kids who had been soundly criticized for being 'overrated,' burst the ball game wide open." Unable to sit still, the crowd jumped up and down when burly Raymon scored off a rebound, driving the Cubs to a two-point lead. Then in rapid-fire succession, Howie, Raymon, Jimmy Jones, and Doodle added other buckets, giving Cuba a ten-point lead with three and a half minutes to go.

In those waning moments, University High started fouling in its attempt to get the ball. But the Cubs figured their lead looked big enough to let Howie have the ball. When he began killing the clock with his dribbling exhibition, the crowd went wild as University High scrambled after the ball with increasing desperation. Cuba won, 57-50, as Doodle took scoring honors with twenty-three points.

Although Doodle and Howie got the lion's share of attention, and justifiably so, what made Cuba so great was the team itself: Jimmy Jones was a fine floor general; Raymon, a great rebounder; Jimmie Webb, another great rebounder and a set-shot artist. Jimmie did a lot of clutch scoring and was an outstanding outside shooter. Joe Buddy was an excellent defensive player. Many times he drew the assignment of guarding the other team's high scorer and was able to limit the opponent's leading scorer. Joe Buddy was a good steady ball handler who made many contributions to the score. Proud of his boys, Coach Story said that year, "I've really got a first six instead of a first five!"

CHAPTER 21

IRREPRESSIBLE AND IRRESISTIBLE

"THE AIM, IF REACHED OR NOT, MAKES GREAT THE LIFE."
—ROBERT BROWNING

Memorial Coliseum—1951. To the people who had never seen them before, the Cubs were hard not to notice and impossible not to admire. More thrilling perhaps than anything else was the way the Cubs' wins came in games where they had to come from behind. Many times when playing a team that was hailed as invincible, Cuba would trail until the fourth quarter. Then, suddenly, they would burst forward, tie the score, push harder and harder and get ahead, winning the game just before the final horn was sounded. The Cubs were determined to win and their sheer will pulled them through to victory many times.

Coach Story was a great defensive coach and taught his team a great pressing defense. He developed and nurtured a belief in them that they could come from behind no matter how far behind they were. He had them believing that they'd find a way to get ahead. They won a lot of close ball games with that philosophy; it became part of their history. When they were behind, they'd think "get in zone," which meant "get on a hitting streak."

Their apparent style—spot the opponent a lead, then wear him down, pull out ahead when he falters, then make him play

157

catch-up—caused terrible anxiety in the spectators, but it was compelling. Whenever the Cubs were trailing, the suspense in the stadium was palpable. The crowd would get overly excited, anxiously
watching for the Cubs to spring ahead in the fourth quarter. Once
they got a couple of points ahead, they'd freeze the ball. When
fouled, they'd take the ball out of bounds and continue to keep it.
They had this technique down perfectly.

Cuba was not the first little team playing in a state tournament
that had captured the attention of basketball fans. In the thirty-five-
year history of Kentucky state tournaments, other little spots like Carr
Creek, Heath, Tolu, Brewers, Brooksville, and Corinth had worked
their way into the limelight. However, those other small school teams
did not have the style and personality that Cuba had. Cuba was
unique, and hard-court fans knew that and loved Cuba.

No one player on any of the tournament teams captured the
crowd's fancy the way Doodle did. Irrepressible and irresistible,
Doodle loved to make people laugh. And laugh they did—at his
behavior, his talk, and his appearance. Although his mother
claimed he ate like he had a tapeworm, he was thin and limber as
a reed, but hard as a brick of clay. His spiky straight dark brown
hair, kept in a crew cut, drew attention to his large ears that
fanned out from the sides of his head. He had a ravine-like cleft
in his chin and a wide crooked smile that evoked a smile in return—a smile that few girls could resist. His brown eyes sparkled
with mischief. When he walked, his arms and legs seemed to dan-
gle from his trunk, making him look gangly and uncoordinated,
but when he got on the hardwood, he was a well-coordinated
runner. Unlike the others, he never appeared tense or nervous.
His comic manner often tossed his opponents off balance psy-
chologically. Many times during a game, an opposing player
could not keep from laughing at Doodle's remarks and antics.
He'd call out to his opponents telling them what he was going to
do. He would point out the place on the floor where he would
shoot to score and then actually score. No other high school
player behaved the way Doodle did. Soon after he arrived in

No player captured the crowd's fancy the way Doodle did. Irrepressible and irresistible, Doodle loved to make people laugh, and his brown eyes sparkled with mischief. (Photo courtesy of Charles Floyd)

Lexington, he became known as "the Comedian." Radio and newspapers christened him "the Prince of Clowns."

Despite all of his foolishness, Doodle was deadly serious about basketball and hell-bent on winning. His phenomenal hook shot, which made him the top scorer in many games, was compared to that of Cliff Hagan's.

Two years older than Doodle, Cliff Hagan had a stunning hook shot that Rupp said was one of the best he had ever seen. While in high school, Hagan had watched Bob Lavoy, who played for Coach Diddle, shoot a hook shot in a game in Bowling Green at Western Kentucky State College. Hagan went home and practiced the shot in his backyard until he perfected it. Even as a youngster, he played basketball with a grace and precision that separated him from other great players. From Owensboro Senior High, he went on to play center for the University of Kentucky, where he paired perfectly with Frank Ramsey, a great rebounder, who loved to intercept passes and run the length of the floor.

Doodle was not trying to imitate Hagan; he had never seen him play. Doodle was just shooting in a way that came naturally to him, and his technique was different from Hagan's. Hagan would position himself on the court, extend his arm way out horizontally from his shoulder, then toss the ball over his head into the basket. Bewildered defenders took to waving their hands furiously in his face to prevent him from looking at the goal to shoot. But Hagan was so extraordinarily good at scoring with this shot that he did not have to look at the goal to send the ball down through the net. From his position on the court, he knew exactly where and how to shoot the ball to score. Incredulous as it might sound, he had perfected his technique to the point that he could make the shot successfully while blindfolded.

Doodle's shot was different but just as remarkable. Positioned deep from the basket, he would lean far into his right side, stretch his arm straight out, back, and down—almost touching the floor. Then he'd bring his arm up in a wide sweeping semicircle movement and with his arm extended straight over his head so that nobody could get the ball, he would shoot the ball for a perfect basket. The fabulous thing was he could make that shot from a great distance with amazing accuracy. Until they watched Doodle perform this feat, cage fans had never seen any other player shoot in that winding fashion. This shot became known as "Doodle's Windmill."

The Cubs were never merely a sentimental favorite, as other small rural teams were; they were a favorite in the strictest sense of the word. Their team differed from other teams in four major ways. First, they played a showier, more spectacular game than any other team. No one had seen another high school boys' basketball team pattern themselves after the Harlem Globetrotters. Second, they introduced a new style of high school boys' basketball: a flashier, much faster manner of playing the game. Although Kentucky high school basketball teams coming out of the 1940s into the 1950s started using the fast break, which made for a much more exciting brand of basketball, fans had never seen high school boys handle the ball the way Cuba handled it. Third, Cuba had so many come-from-behind wins that were nerve-wracking and gut-wrenching to watch but so thrilling. Fourth, although the Cubs were showmen, they were, as their opponents discovered, well-grounded in the fundamentals and hard to beat. Opponents and fans never knew what to expect from them.

Ed Diddle, one of the most colorful college coaches ever, was in the coliseum the night Cuba beat University High, and immediately after the game he sought out Jack Story, getting right in Story's face, pulling on his coat collar with both hands, asking him in that quirky manner of speech Diddle was famous for: "That Crittenden boy—he dribble that ball like that all the time? And Doodle, he throw that ball like that all that time?" Coach Story laughed, "Yessir, they sure do!"

At 3:00 P.M. on Saturday, the Cubs played Whitesburg, whose star was Jim Toliver, a great scorer. During the opening half, the Cubs were true to form. They fell behind in the first period, then ate away at Whitesburg's lead but trailed, 32-29, at halftime. In the second half they would presumably grind Whitesburg down.

But Whitesburg refused to follow the script and instead ran out to a ten-point lead.

Cuba had to fight throughout the last half. With one minute left the Cubs held a one-point lead. Finally, they intercepted a Whitesburg pass and threw the ball to Doodle. As he was going in for a layup, he was fouled. After making his one foul shot, he took the ball out of bounds, the Cubs stalled the last few seconds, and won, 65-62. The fans rose to their feet, blowing horns, throwing confetti, and chanting "Cuba! Cuba! All the Way!"

In the afterglow of that game, the Cubs felt a lingering weariness. It had been a draining contest, and they were not a deep team. Howie and Doodle got no rest during games and the other starters got very little. Playing three tournament games in three days was grueling work. At tournament games, the opposing teams had substitutes who were nearly as good as the starters, not like the ones the Cubs played in the county games, where the "Jimmies" who went in as replacements were no challenge at all. Here at the coliseum every single player was good. Before the final game at 8:45 P.M. with Clark County, the Cubs had had only four hours of rest—not enough to restore their strength after just playing that afternoon thriller with Whitesburg. Clark County was a powerful team that had beaten Cuba earlier that year by one point. The Cubs were not up to facing the Cardinals again that night.

In this championship game, Clark County took off with ease and rolled up a 16-3 advantage. But Cuba had lagged behind that far before and come back to win, so fans anxiously waited for the burst of energy that was so characteristic of Cuba. But it never came. By the close of the first quarter, Howie and Raymon had carved the margin down to 18-10, but the Cardinals were controlling the boards and getting almost all of the rebounds. Clark County led by as many as sixteen in the second quarter and went to the locker room with a 36-23 halftime lead.

The Cubs were visibly weary in the second half. Clark County had three big players who had valuable tournament experience: Lewis Snowden, Bobo Pelfrey, and Linville Puckett. Doodle said that trying to move the six-foot-five Lewis Snowden was like trying to move a mountain. Snowden played brilliantly during the first half, scoring fifteen points. But in the second half, he collected four personal fouls, as did Cubs guard Jimmy Jones. Clark County's experience and power overwhelmed the weary inexperienced Cubs. The Cardinals kept going full steam ahead in the second half, and it was obvious that the little "comeback" team was not coming back this time. Final score: Clark County, 69; Cuba, 44.

Nevertheless, the Cuba Cubs had achieved something special. They had come from nowhere to become the runner-up team in the 1951 Kentucky State Boys' Basketball Tournament. It had been a great season, an unbelievable 36-3 season. But in their minds, they had failed.

CHAPTER 22

GROWING
INTO LIONS

"PRIDE GOETH FORTH ON HORSEBACK, GRAND AND GAY; BUT COMETH BACK
ON FOOT AND BEGS ITS WAY."

—LONGFELLOW

Cuba, Kentucky—1951–1952. The Cubs kept their promise about building their endurance. They ran and practiced basketball all summer long. The Cuba and Pilot Oak villagers watched them with admiration as they streaked across fields chasing rabbits. By January 1952 they were actually *catching* rabbits.

Many mornings before school, Howie and Doodle would run from their homes in Pilot Oak to Wrays three miles away, where Ted Bradley and Jimmie Webb lived. Then all four of them would run to Cuba four miles down the road and would beat the school bus to the school. In the evenings sometimes, they'd run ten miles to Mayfield and back. Every afternoon they practiced in the gym. All this was done without prompting from Coach Story.

One month before basketball season started, they began running up and down the bleachers fifty times and around the gym sixty times a day. Then after school they'd run to Harper's, two miles round-trip from the school. On every nice day they ran down country roads. On weekends Doodle and Howie would run up and down the Murray road every morning and then play one-on-one in

Howie and Joe Buddy get in a little R&R at the beach in the summer of 1951 before returning for one more year of Cuba basketball. (Photo courtesy of Joe Buddy Warren)

Pilot Oak in front of the store. Nothing, absolutely nothing, was going to keep them from being stronger and better should they make it to the state tournament that year. They even stopped smoking. They were heading toward basketball season with a confidence and enthusiasm that sometimes got them into trouble with their teachers.

By October Howie, Doodle, Joe Buddy, Ted, Harold, Jimmie Webb, and Jimmy Brown, along with a few others, had to be placed in a special class because their mischief in Mr. Dowell's agriculture class had been so distracting that Mr. Dowell refused to let them continue. In plain language the teacher told Coach Story to figure out what to do with *"your* boys" because he was having nothing to do with them from then on—basketball stars or not.

165

For a couple of days, a grim-faced Coach Story went about his work annoyed for being put in such an unflattering position. He was angry with the boys and with Mr. Dowell. There was no other class for the boys to take that period and no other teacher available to teach agriculture. He could not send them to study hall because they needed a credit class.

One morning after Coach Story passed Mrs. Sandifer, the home economics teacher, it dawned on him that he could create a special home economics class that she could instruct. Although Mrs. Sandifer was barely five feet tall and hardly weighed ninety pounds, she was a figure of authority. In fact, she was a despot who had absolute control over her classroom. Her subject matter included manners and speech. No one in her class was allowed to say such things as "idinit" for *isn't* it, or "yesterdee" for *yesterday*, or "Babdist" for *Baptist* or "ovair thar" for *over there*. Nobody, including Doodle, Ted, or Joe Buddy, ever teased her the way they did the other teachers.

At the first meeting of this newly formed class, Mrs. Sandifer told the basketball players what she expected them to do and how and when they were going to do it. No questions and no discussion. The moment she turned her back, Jimmie Webb started whispering and giggling to Ted, not knowing that Mrs. Sandifer's peripheral vision was even better than Howie's. Surprising the thunder out of Jimmie, she reached out, yanked a thatch of his curly hair, and pulled it as hard as she could. He thought she was going to jerk his scalp off. She made a vivid impression on him that day and after that incident he behaved.

Mrs. Sandifer's class turned out to be one of the boys' best, and she, their favorite teacher. They learned to cook, serve food, preserve foods, make beds, tie a necktie, set a table, wash and iron, clean house, mend clothes, sew a little, and many other practical skills.

The Cuba school had no classes in drama, glee club, band, or art, and it never sponsored formal proms or dances (Cuba believed that dancing was a sin). So for recreation, Doodle, Howie, Mason Harris, and Jimmie Webb formed a quartet, singing gospel music mostly, with Mary Nell Morris playing the piano for them. They entered an FFA talent contest in nearby Benton, Kentucky, and they came in second.

The fall of 1951 Doodle and his friends buzzed around the county in a '36 Chevy he bought for twenty-three dollars from Mutt Johnson in Cuba. He bought it with money he had earned in Detroit, where he had worked for a few weeks that summer. Like

Each one of Cuba's senior class officers in 1951–52 had close ties to the basketball team: Pictured left to right are class reporter Howie Crittenden, treasurer Martha (Casey) Webb, president Donald Poyner, secretary Carolyn Work, and vice president Joe Buddy Warren. (Cuba school yearbook photo)

his older brother's car, this car had no chassis—no hood, no windshield, no doors, no trunk, no running board, no lights. It was the shell of a car with only a motor, a radiator, a steering wheel, a front and back seat. Nonetheless, the car brought them much happiness. Dressed in clean shirts, blue jeans, and white touring caps that they had bought in Mayfield, the boys felt they were on top of the world. They would load the car with their girlfriends, who thought the old heap was grand, too, and drive all over Graves County. On Saturday nights, as many as six or eight would pile in at one time, and off they'd go to Mayfield to Story's Drive-In, known as the "passion pit," and drive back at night with no lights. They didn't have to worry about hitting other vehicles, though, because hardly any automobiles were ever on the roads in Cuba or Pilot Oak at night. People in the country went to bed just after dusk. There was still no electricity in most places and nowhere to go.

Although Coach Story was pleased with them and their efforts to improve their skills, they often made him angry, especially when he thought they were getting arrogant. Although he wanted them to be confident and proud of their achievements, he could not tolerate excessive pride, or what he called "biggity people." He had a quiet way of handling the ones who were getting bigheaded. At one point, when Jimmie Webb's head began to swell and he went into a slump, Coach Story started taking him out of games. Thinking that he was "just too darn good to be taken out," Jimmie asserted himself. He told Coach Story that if he didn't get more playing time, he was going to quit the team. Coach Story replied, "Well, Webb, you just go ahead and quit." As he turned to walk away, he added, "But you can be cocksure that I'll draw my paycheck just the same."

One time the starters got into serious trouble for playing hooky, an incident that created a real ruckus at school. According to school policy, if you didn't show up for school in the morning, there was no problem; you were simply counted as absent. If you came in at noon, you'd be counted absent only a half day. But if you ever left the school ground after you arrived, you were in big trouble. Leaving the school ground without permission was, in Coach Story's mind, equivalent to a felony.

One morning Doodle, Jimmie, Joe Buddy, Ted, Raymon, and Howie arrived at school early—long before all of the teachers were there. It was a summer-like autumn morning—cool, clear, and beautiful. Thinking that it was too nice a day to stay inside, they decided to race the ten miles to Mayfield to get haircuts and play a little pool. They were in an especially joyful mood: The semester was nearly over, the Christmas holidays and the invitational, district, and regional tournaments were coming up soon. Although they knew how seriously Coach Story disapproved of any student playing hooky, they figured that he and the teachers would not care so much now that the Cubs were seniors and graduating that spring. And after all, the Cubs had it fixed in their minds that they were the exceptions—they were going to be 1952 state champions. Besides that, they figured as long as they got back by noon for ball practice Coach Story might not even miss them.

Older than the others, Raymon, who was nearly twenty and married, presented a kind of big-brother image. He was always trying to keep the others out of trouble. At one of the Christmas tournaments, when someone gave the Cubs a bottle of wine, Raymon drank it all, saying that he did not want Doodle, Howie, Webb, and Joe Buddy to get into trouble. He'd do anything he could to keep the others from doing something that Coach Story would not like. He never wanted to do anything that might make Coach Story angry. He had done that once in the ninth grade and never forgot the paddling that Coach Story gave him. So Raymon tried to talk the others out of skipping. But Joe Buddy, Ted, and Doodle tossed his advice away as if it were a cigarette butt and assured him that Coach Story was not going to paddle them. After all, they were too old for that kind of thing now. If he did anything at all, Joe Buddy said confidently, he'd give them three days' suspension. Ted chirped cheerily, "Wouldn't that be a swell vacation? Come on and go! Raymon, we're nineteen years old and, why, hell, man, you're married. He won't paddle a *married* man." Raymon left school unconvinced and refused to go with them. He'd be back at noon for practice, he said.

After classes started that morning, Coach Story rounded the corners of the school building looking for his team. He had gotten a glimpse of Joe Buddy earlier, so he figured the others had been to school, too. When he couldn't find them, he sent Jess Warren to search for them. By then the whole high school student body, about 130 students, knew that the starters had skipped, and they giggled with glee and excitement thinking about the repercussions that surely would ensue.

Without any delay, Jess found the boys in Watson's Pool Room in Mayfield. The moment they saw him walk in, their mood shifted from hilarity to panic. The drive back to Cuba was a silent one. When they got in sight of the school, they saw a jut-jawed Coach Story planted solidly in front of the building, waiting for them. He scowled as they got out of the car and started toward him. In a throaty voice, he commanded, "Dress for practice and go to my office." Joe Buddy flinched and began stuttering, "But, Mr. Story, sir, we were just going to get a haircut, sir, and then come right back, sir. We were going to come right back, yes, sir." Coach Story's anger deepened and his stare sent shivers into the boy.

His office was no larger than six by ten feet, and his desk and three wooden straight-back chairs took up most of the room. A few awards, pictures of his wife and children, and his bachelor's degree from Murray were hanging crookedly on the walls. In the corner near the door was a metal coat rack piled with his old jackets and hats. In another corner on the floor were his mud-caked work boots and dingy basketball shoes. The wall behind his desk was lined with bookshelves, stacked mostly with magazines and newspapers. The only window was wide and halfway covered with a soiled white shade.

The first thing the boys saw, much to their regret, was the wooden paddle lying across his desk. This "principal's paddle" was about twenty-eight inches long and about three-quarters of an inch thick. It was one that Coach Story himself had made out of hickory wood. It angled narrowly down on one end to provide his hand a good grip; the other end widened to about twelve inches across. The most mysterious thing was how he managed to hide that paddle from everyone, including his friend Jess Warren. The location had to be kept secret or else some boy would have surely stolen the paddle and thrown it in the huge potbelly stove that heated the gym.

Facing Coach Story, the boys stood erect with their hands clasped behind their backs and feet spread apart. The coach leaned back in his chair, crossed his legs, and folded his arms over his chest. He stared at them for a full minute. Then he reached over to the right side of his desk and flicked the switch on the new intercom system, permitting the entire high school faculty and student body to listen to what was going on in his office. Knowing that was to happen really embarrassed them. He began by saying, "Well, boys, according to the school policy for skipping school, you have the option of a three-day suspension or five licks with this paddle."

Sighing with relief that the five licks were not going to be an automatic punishment, Joe Buddy announced that he'd take the suspension and reached for the door knob to leave. But Coach Story reached over and pulled Joe Buddy's hand away from the door knob, saying, "I don't think so. I think you all *prefer* the five licks." His unexpected words sent pangs of fear through them. With games coming up, the coach was not about to let them lose three days of practice.

Without any discussion, he took off his coat, unbuttoned his collar, and loosened his tie as the boys exchanged horrified glances. He opened the door and instructed them to line up in alphabetical order. "Bradley, you're first. Stay here!" he ordered. "The rest of you get out and wait your turn."

Jess waited anxiously with them. Jimmie recalled, "We were wearing just our T-shirts and practice trunks and had nothing to block the blows. Coach Story had us bend over his desk so he could whack us hard. The pain was terrible. He was a strong man. His hands were like bear paws, and he could swing that paddle, too. He blistered our rear ends that day." Although the boys held

171

back their yells because they did not want the other students to hear them, Jess cried like a baby while Joe Buddy was taking his punishment. The hilarity of it was grand and then, just as it is now, kids love to see other kids get their comeuppance.

By the time Coach Story had finished doling out the punishment, Raymon, not knowing what had happened, returned to school. Carrying his little green satchel that contained his practice outfit and shoes, Raymon was scurrying toward the gym, when Coach Story spotted him and refused to listen to his explanation. As the other boys sat on the bleachers laughing so hard they cried, Raymon followed the coach into the office. When he walked out, Raymon still had his little green satchel tucked under his arm, but he was really stepping high and gingerly. His rear end was on fire, his face was dark red as a beet, his eyes were bugged out, and the veins in his neck were swollen; Raymon was angry. When the others saw him, they doubled over with laughter, making him even angrier.

CHAPTER 23

FAITHFUL TO A VOW

"ALL THINGS ARE WON BY DILIGENCE."

—MENANDER

Cuba, Kentucky—1951–1952. Their senior school year, the Cubs, unfortunately, paid little attention to their school-work. They couldn't. It was impossible. Coach Story had completely revised their schedule, so that they played one game after another. In addition to playing all the area schools in Graves County, they played in invitational tournaments across the state, plus many charity games. And they played the top teams in the state of Kentucky and also the number one and two teams in Tennessee.

They opened the 1951–52 season with four quick wins over Wingo, 82-36; Farmington, 72-34; Fancy Farm, 120-18; and Columbia, 76-50. In November 1951 they traveled to Maysville, in northern Kentucky, clear across the state, where they won the Burley Invitational Tobacco Bowl Tournament by beating Carrollton, 60-43, in the opening round, and Inez, 75-52, for the championship. Doodle was in complete control of his shooting and rebounding in this tournament, and he played defense superbly. In the Carrollton game, he was the leading scorer with twenty-seven points, followed by Howie with thirteen, Bill Pollock with six, and Raymon and Jimmie each with four; Harold Roberts contributed three and Joe Buddy added two.

In the championship game against Inez, the Cubs played a splendid floor game and controlled the backboards just as they had done with Carrollton. During this game Doodle performed, as the local sportswriters described, "spectacularly." Having never seen the boy's hook shot, they were immensely impressed and called his technique "a weird, unique, winding windmill sort of movement." Doodle connected repeatedly with this shot and led all scorers with twenty-nine points, helping the Cubs forge ahead at the outset of the second period. Shooting from the perimeter and driving to the basket, Howie collected seventeen points of his own. He put the Cubs ahead by fifteen during the second half with a quick, behind-the-back dribble around the man guarding him and then speedily driving to the basket for an uncontested layup. Jimmie contributed thirteen points in the Inez game; Joe Buddy, six; Bill Pollock, four; Raymon and Paul Simpson, two each.

The Cubs returned to the regular season schedule and kept winning. Their victories included wins over Saint Mary's, 64-41; Metropolis, Illinois, 54-47; Lowes, 92-36; Brewers, 74-60; Symsonia, 86-56; Henderson's Holy Name, 47-30, thus improving the Cubs' 1951–52 record to 12-0. Next they won the Paducah Invitational Christmas Championship Tournament by defeating Crittenden County, 86-48; Bandana, 70-61; and the highly regarded Lone Oak, 72-54. Beating Lone Oak was especially sweet. Coached by Don Stephenson, Lone Oak had an excellent ball club that year. Sonny Hubbs, "Slick" Herndon, Tommy Stephenson, and six-foot-seven Ken Donaldson were all outstanding players. But that night they were no match for Cuba. Doodle, who was recovering from the flu, scored only nine points, but Howie led with twenty-seven and Joe Buddy added twelve.

The night they played the Lone Oak game was a good example of Coach Story's flexibility. For some reason (probably because of their overpowering sense of superiority at that point), the Cubs decided they were not going to dribble the ball the first half. And they did not. The ball did not touch the floor; they just passed it. Although they were just barely ahead, Coach Story never said a word to them. They won the game but not by as many points as they could have.

After they whipped Lowes, 116-49, for their sixteenth straight victory, the Cubs proceeded to the Purchase-Pennyrile Basketball Tournament at Murray. In the first game Wickliffe handed Cuba its first loss of the season, 52-51. The Cubs chalked their defeat up to bad luck: Raymon, with sore ankles, was not up to speed, and Howie and Jimmie Webb were suffering from the flu. The Cubs then played Henderson's Holy Name in the consolation game, winning, 71-56.

The regular-season schedule picked up again with the Cubs going against Sedalia, winning, 59-41. That Friday they traveled the long trip to Lexington, where they again lost, 48-41, to Manual, one of the largest schools in the state. In that game Doodle badly injured his ankle. The next morning they went on to Horse Cave to play Caverna. But they were down physically because Raymon had caught a nasty cold, and Doodle with his swollen ankle was able to play only about a half. Everyone wondered how he managed to last that long. Still, the Cubs inched passed Caverna, 36-31.

After playing eight games in nine days, Cuba was scheduled to meet Selmer, Tennessee's number-one team, in the Fifteenth Annual Mayfield Charities Invitational Tournament. Every contest Cuba played in western Kentucky was a sellout game. But this clash with Selmer created such a furor that fire marshal Bill Cloar said he wished he could "push all four walls of the high school gym back so that a couple thousand or more Cuba-Selmer fans could see the game." Only 1,750 people could be seated in the gym, and after that many tickets were sold, the gate was shut down. Cloar said that 5,000 tickets could have easily been sold.

Several hundred supporters from the little Tennessee community of Selmer accompanied its team to Mayfield, and among those attending that night was Western Kentucky coach Ed Diddle. The Tennessee newspapers, promoting the game as a charity benefit, announced, "The Lions should provide Jack Story's quintet with a real test—as they feature a fast break attack combined with speed

Ann Dick Hainline was Cuba's Senior Basketball Queen of
1951–52, and Jackie Saxon was Junior Basketball Queen. (Cuba
school yearbook photo)

and lots of rebound power." Coached by Jerry Smith, a graduate
of Lambuth College in Jackson, Tennessee, Selmer's Lions had a
reputation for being extremely aggressive and speedy. With its
string of fifty-three consecutive victories, Selmer was banking on an
undefeated season that year.

Jack Story was jittery the night of the game. He knew that the
Lions resembled the Cave-in-Rock quintet who had surprised him
the year before, beating his team in the Paducah Invitational Tournament. He wanted so badly to beat Selmer because Selmer was
highly rated, but he feared his team might be too tired that night
to do so. He knew that he had been pushing them too hard in the
past two weeks. They had traveled to Lexington Friday and then on

to Horse Cave the following night. Raymon was still sick, and Doodle's injured ankle was bluish black and swollen the size of a grapefruit. Coach Story knew that there was no way Doodle could play at 100 percent in the Selmer game, and he was hoping that Howie could carry the extra heavy load that night.

Selmer had scouted Cuba and saw for itself what the newspapers had been hailing as "Cuba's scoring twins." So when Selmer faced Cuba, they doubled up on Howie and Doodle, leaving Jimmie Webb, Joe Buddy, and Bill Pollock nearly open. Taking advantage of the situation, Joe Buddy connected early in the game with a set shot from twenty-five feet, and from that moment on, the Cubs were in command all the way. Jimmie Webb scored fifteen points in the first half and by halftime, the lead was Cuba's, 40-23.

In disbelief and despair, Selmer fans sat tearfully, wringing their hands as they watched the Cubs collect their twentieth victory of the season against two losses, 69-50. Despite his sore ankle, Doodle kept capturing the ball as it bounced off the boards while Selmer players swarmed around him. Offensively, Doodle made brilliant windmill shots from all sections of the court and racked up twenty-four points. Jimmie ripped the net on set shots and scored nineteen. Howie also made nineteen—all in the last half. Joe Buddy added four and Raymon three. Both Joe and Raymon put in good performances in the first half, but Joe fouled out early in the second half and Raymon, with four personal fouls, sat on the bench much of the time. Bill, Harold, Ted, and Jimmy Brown came through in supportive style. The Lions could not penetrate Cuba's defense, and the Cubs moved to an easy victory. In the closing ceremony that night, Ed Diddle, accompanied by Kelly Thompson, assistant to the president at Western Kentucky, presented a handsome trophy to Coach Story.

Returning to regular-season action, Cuba won over Symsonia, 58-42, on January 22, and the following night beat Warren County, 64-38. Next came the Louisville Invitational Tournament where the Cubs beat Louisville Male, 63-50, and Campbellsville,

48-44, only to lose to Louisville Manual in the finals, 70-58, for their third loss of the season. By now Raymon's cold had infected Howie and Jimmie Webb, and Doodle's ankle was still swollen and sore. It was no wonder they lost again at Allen County, 49-48, with four starters disabled.

Despite their health problems, the Cubs redeemed themselves for an earlier loss by beating Wickliffe, 68-33, but Wickliffe was playing without its star player, Phil Rollins, who was injured. The Cubs next played Humbolt, Tennessee, and won, 74-52, but then lost to Clark County, 57-48. The final game of the 1952 regular

Cuba cheerleaders Barbara Harper, Carolyn Work, and Martha (Casey) Webb rest their vocal chords outside Harper's Grocery. (Photo courtesy of Donald Poyner)

season ended with their win, again, over Lone Oak, 67-62. They entered the district tournament play with a record of 27-5.

The Cubs won the district tournament by defeating Farmington, 70-35; Wingo, 88-58; and Symsonia, 67-36.

In the opening game of the 1952 regional tournament, Cuba stomped Clinton, 74-29, and then whipped Symsonia in the semifinals, 61-34, to advance to the finals against Wickliffe. They played a great defensive game and defeated Wickliffe, 54-42, even with a healthy Phil Rollins back in the lineup for the opposition. With their victory over Wickliffe, the Cubs had again earned a ticket to the state tournament. Even with his ankle still sore, Doodle did not slow down. He led the scoring against Wickliffe with twenty-four points, making eight field goals in the second half, most of them coming on his trademark windmill shots. As usual, Howie stunned the crowd with his fancy ball-handling act and added fourteen points. Jimmie Webb contributed eight more.

Unlike the 1950–51 season, this season had been a real struggle. As seniors, they had suffered many injuries and illnesses. They had already lost Jimmy Jones, their excellent floor general, who had graduated the previous May. On the other hand, they had gained Bill Pollock, a definite asset, as well as Jimmy Brown, a great substitute center, and Harold Roberts, a strong forward. Their victories had always been team victories and always would be. The Cuba Cubs then advanced to the 1952 state tournament with a 33-5 record.

Kentucky basketball fans watched with a heightened sense of anticipation.

CHAPTER 24

THE COMEBACK KIDS

"OPEN THE GATES AND GIVE THE VICTORS WAY."

—SHAKESPEARE

Lexington, Kentucky—March 1952. On Wednesday, March 19, the day the tournament was to begin, Lexington sportswriter Larry Shropshire in his column "Down in Front" for the *Lexington Leader* reminded his readers that "it would be a fine thing if (the criticism from visiting school people and team followers) could be avoided this week and in future tournaments. . . . The colorful team from distant Cuba . . . was inadvertently and unintentionally the hub of the trouble [complaints heard after the 1951 tournament], with certainly no blame whatsoever to be attached to those lads."

Shropshire continued:

Catching the fancy of the crowd on their first trip to the state meet, the Cubs suddenly, and quite unexpectedly, no doubt, had acquired a tremendous and very noisy rooting section. They could do no wrong, in the eyes of the tourney throngs, and their opponents could do no right, or at least nothing to receive the approval of the noisy majority of the onlookers. Cuba picked up more well-wishers and more vocal support than any other team competing in a Kentucky tournament ever had, and that surely was all right until the cheering for the Cubs reached the point where it was almost fanatical—much to the distress and pained concern of players and supporters of the opposing team.

Not only were the loud cheers for the favorites offensive, but also the boos and yells at officials whenever they made calls against the Cubs. Cuba rooters were rude and hurt the feelings of players on the other teams. "Feelings reached the point where the tourney crowd even strongly opposed the local entry, University High, in its game with Cuba. . . . Such rabid partisanship displayed by some tourney crowds last year" should be avoided this time around.

His advice, however, went unheeded. Cuba's return to Memorial Coliseum was like a homecoming. Cage fans immediately embraced the Cubs, and even the press gave them a warm welcome. Sportswriters were saying much the same as the editor of the *Paducah Sun-Democrat* did: "No University of Kentucky basketball team ever got the reception in the Coliseum that the Cubs got Friday and Saturday nights."

In the opening game of the 1952 state tournament, the Cubs went up against Corbin, rated stronger than any of the teams Cuba had defeated at the state tournament the year before. Corbin's Red Hounds were powered by Jerry Bird, a big center whom many then described as the best college prospect in the state.

At the start it looked as if this might be a close game all the way. The teams traded baskets through four early ties before the Red Hounds moved out to an 18-14 lead after one quarter, on the strength of Bird's thirteen points. The Cubs tried everything they could to control Corbin's big center, but with little success. It was beginning to look as if he might whip the Cubs single-handedly. Still, there were a full three quarters to go, and the Cubs weren't out of tricks.

Cuba's go-to guy in the first half turned out to be Jimmie Webb. Behind Webb's six-of-six shooting from the field, the Cubs stayed within striking distance in the first half. Although Corbin led by as many as seven points in the second quarter, Cuba closed the gap to 34-32 at intermission. It still was anybody's game at that point because the Cubs finally managed to shoot down Bird, holding him to two second-quarter points.

As had become their trademark over the last two seasons, the Cubs still trailed well into the second half. Corbin held the edge pretty steadily because of its superiority on the boards. With Corbin still ahead, 47-42, entering the fourth quarter, the big question for Cuba was Doodle. Saddled with two fouls less than a minute into the game, he had not been his usual aggressive self, choosing instead to play cautious defense instead of risking any further foul trouble. But time was running out for the Cubs. After Joe Buddy hit a crip shot making the score 47-44, he then missed a pair of free throws that could have cut Corbin's lead to one early in the fourth quarter. Doodle took over and again played with typical abandon. He hit with a one-handed shot that put Cuba within one point of Corbin. That was only the beginning. Doodle then hit a wide hook shot with several Corbin players hanging on him. Two more Doodle hook shots later, Cuba was in the lead, 52-49, and there were just a little more than four minutes left in the game.

With Doodle breaking loose for the basket and being fed the ball by Howie's pinpoint passing, the score rose to 58-51 in the last two minutes. Using his windmill hook shot, Doodle hit six straight baskets and scored twelve of his twenty-two points in the last quarter. Joe Buddy added two points for good measure. As Cuba pulled away for a 60-53 victory, with Howie killing the clock late with more of his dazzling dribbling, the coliseum crowd went delirious with joy! The Cubs had come from behind again just as they had done the year before in three games against Covington Holmes, Lexington University High, and Whitesburg.

Cuba's next opponent a night later would be Henry Clay of Lexington, a team that had advanced to the quarterfinals with a victory over College High, 62-52. For a change, Cuba found a way to win without falling behind for most of the game. After Henry Clay's

Howie was a great ball handler who wasn't afraid of taking it to the hoop, either, as he does here in a 1952 state tournament game against Henry Clay. (*Lexington Herald-Leader* photo courtesy of Howie Crittenden)

star guard Bob "Sugar" Anderson scored the game's first points, the Cubs quickly came back to take an early lead and stayed in front the rest of the way. Although Henry Clay came within three points several times during the first quarter, it couldn't stop Cuba's offensive play. Cuba led at the end of the first period, 16-11, behind Doodle's ten points.

In the second quarter Cuba increased its lead to 23-13 thanks to Joe Buddy's two jump shots and Jimmie Webb's three-point play off an offensive rebound. The Cubs stayed in front anywhere from eight to eleven points the rest of the quarter and ended the half ahead, 36-26.

There had even been some time for comic relief, featuring, of course, Doodle. At one point in the second quarter, he split his pants, called a time-out, and rushed to the dressing room. When he returned sporting a new pair of shorts, the crowd broke out into laughter.

But Cuba's laughter was short-lived. Before the half was over, Jimmie Webb had already fouled out, and Raymon, one of Cuba's best rebounding hopes, had been forced to the bench with a twisted ankle. With more than a half still to play, Coach Story was in the position of having to utilize his bench more than usual, although Bill Pollock and Harold Roberts performed admirably in replacing Jimmie Webb and Raymon, respectively.

During the third quarter the Blue Devils started to rally and cut Cuba's lead to seven points, but Howie made several baskets to get the lead back into double digits, 40-29. Scrappy Henry Clay fought hard and pruned the margin to four points but couldn't do anything with Cuba's offensive play. Moving in and taking control, Doodle made two hook shots with two minutes left in the quarter and Cuba had a 46-41 lead. Shooting one basket after another, Anderson and Duff put Henry Clay within two points, but then Doodle made a free throw and Howie, a tip-in. The period ended with Cuba ahead, 49-44.

Early in the fourth quarter, Howie dribbled right through the entire Lexington team for a layup. Doodle drove in for a crip shot, and Raymon hit a set shot, to up the lead to 55-44. Cuba went into a semistall for the remainder of the game. Henry Clay fouled in several attempts to get the ball back, but Cuba refused the free-throw attempts and opted to keep possession of the ball. The Cubs' victory over Henry Clay, 61-47, moved them into the semifinals where they would play Hindman on Saturday.

Because the majority of those attending the games, including many of those from Lexington, were enthusiastically rooting for Cuba, the few cheering for Henry Clay could barely be seen but not heard. In an article two days earlier, the *Lexington Leader* sportswriter Larry Shropshire had pointed out to his readers that such "rabid support" for one team is "hurtful," and that teams opposing Cuba are made to feel as if they "were guilty of some heinous crime." The cheers for Cuba's opponents were drowned out by the louder Cuba fans. And officials making a call against Cuba were booed practically off the court. During the 1951 state tournament, the supporters of other teams, Shropshire wrote, "naturally resent the treatment accorded their athletes and probably worked up a slow burn about Lexington as a place to compete." The day before the final games were to be played, Shropshire, disgruntled with the coliseum crowd's behavior, wrote a column that indicated his attitude toward Cuba had soured, and he especially directed his wrath at Howie. He wrote: "Spend just a little time on the sidelines at the Crittenden Circus—that's what the state high school tournament will have to be called as long as Cuba's Howie Crittenden is participating, the master ball handler being a super-show-off as well and relegating everything else save his own performance to the category of sideshow attractions—and it becomes obvious that one change in the rules would make basketball a 100 percent better game. Stop these silly and almost continual marches from one foul line to the other while actual competition is held up. . . ."

When someone showed Shropshire's article to Howie, the boy was shocked at first and then devastated by the columnist's insults. While playing his heart out during the games, he had been suffering from a toothache, and he felt bad enough without learning what had been written about him. Trying to console him, his

A prominent newspaper story that labeled Howie "a show-off" for
his ball-handling abilities missed the whole point—he was a rare
breed of high school basketball player who could kill lots of clock and
control games in the spirit of the rules at the time. (*Lexington
Herald-Leader* photo courtesy of Howie Crittenden)

teammates urged him to ignore the remarks. Doodle growled,
"Don't you give a rat's tail for what that piss ant writes."

Many tournament regulars wrote to the paper responding to
Shropshire's article and saying much the same as Oliver Wagoner
Jr. said in his letter: "If Crittenden is such a show-off and cannot
play ball, why doesn't some of the 'good' ball teams show up? Crittenden, 'The Show-Off' did fairly well against Henry Clay, and I
didn't see Anderson, or any of the other players on this 'better'
team taking the ball away from him."

Wagoner's letter went on to say, "I have no gripe against
the teams, it is just their self-assigned defenders. When Cuba

first came to the tournament last year, they were given a big write-up about where they were from and their watching the Harlem Globetrotters' films, copying their style of play from them. This was for the public and they ate it up. From then on everyone backed Cuba to the hilt, even in defeat they were great. Then Cuba beat a Lexington team, brother, that was all as far as the Lexington papers were concerned. When you say fans should support the 'local' team in the tournament you are talking through your hat. A state tournament has no local team. The teams and the fans come from all over the state and the fans come to see and support the teams of their choice. Also, who are you to tell all these fans that they shouldn't give Cuba their support, which they so justly deserve and, to put it bluntly, yell for whomever they damn please."

Jack Anderson, editor at the *Paducah Sun Democrat*, pointed out that Shropshire was certainly alone in making slurring comments about Howie, for "the hundred or more sports writers and radio announcers covering the tournament voted Crittenden the best player in the meet. . . . Now maybe we're all wrong and Mr. Shropshire is right. . . . Maybe Ed Diddle, Harlan Hodges, and several more big name coaches are all wet, too. . . . All they'd give for Crittenden's services would be their eye teeth. . . . Howie Crittenden is a great basketball player, a modest youth with a burning desire to win, and a gentleman. . . . With all respect to Doodle, Raymon, Joe, and Jimmie, the Cubs couldn't have won without the services of Crittenden. The youngster broke into tears when he read the slurring remarks hurled at him by the Lexington sports writer, who chose to take his wrath out on a youngster fighting his heart out to bring glory to his TEAM, not himself."

After all that excitement Friday night, Doodle was up late, sitting on the sill of the tall window in their room in the Phoenix Hotel. He was looking out over the city as he smoked his cigar. Jimmie Webb and Raymon, sharing the room, were already in bed asleep. Howie whispered, "Doodle, come on to bed. You gotta get some rest. We gotta play tomorrow. We gotta rest."

Doodle answered, "I can't, Howie. I'm as wide awake as a turkey on a turkey shoot."

Called the "battling babies" because it was a young mountain team without seniors, Hindman was under terrific pressure, being well aware of Cuba's growing reputation. It was impossible for them to ignore the crowd's support for Cuba. In the opening moments of the semifinal game, Doodle, relaxed and happy, delighted fans and disarmed the Hindman players and their rooters by shouting, "Praise the Lord! And pass me that ball!" The crowd laughed, knowing that he was capitalizing on the words of a song that had been popular during World War II, "Praise the Lord and Pass the Ammunition!"

That game turned out to be one of the most excruciatingly even contests in the history of the state tournament. Some spectators got so nervous that they could not watch the game anymore and left the bleachers to wait outside. Martha Casey Webb was sitting with her sister Helen and Helen's husband, Herschel, who was Doodle's brother. Unable to watch his baby brother on court, Herschel buried his face in his hands and tried to cover his ears. Then, unable to remain inside the arena, he stood up and told Helen, "I just can't stand it any longer. I gotta get out of here." Helen stayed with Martha but covered her face with her scarf. The Cubs' biggest lead in the first quarter was only four points and their lead at the end of the quarter was 11-8. At halftime the two teams were tied, 19-19.

The third quarter was a thriller; Cuba took some short leads for the first four minutes, but then Hindman moved out ahead, 29-28, when Garnard Martin made another basket from the circle. With thirty-five seconds to go, Jimmie Webb put Cuba ahead, 34-33. But the quarter ended in a 37-37 tie, and it was nip and tuck after that. In the fourth quarter, Jimmie Webb scored a basket and Joe Buddy a free throw. The Cubs went into a stall, letting Howie dribble for two minutes to most of the spectators' delight. With 3:30 to go, Doodle then made a windmill shot to put Cuba up, 42-37. But Joe Martin brought Hindman back, netting a free throw and then stealing the ball from Howie for a layup that made it 42-40.

As Cuba was trying to stall, Martin again got the ball with 1:19 remaining and passed it to Wayne Conley, who missed his shot, and a jump ball resulted. The ball was tipped to Crittenden, who threw it away on a long pass. Joe Buddy then fouled Garnard Martin with fifty-one seconds left. Instead of taking the ball out, Hindman let Martin shoot his foul shots: He made both, tying the game, 42-42. Both teams had chances to score with the seconds ticking away in the fourth quarter, but neither could convert. Joe Buddy's last-second shot from ten feet behind the circle hit the rim and bounced off. Overtime!

No one scored in the first three-minute, sudden-death over-time. But in the second sudden-death overtime, Jimmie Webb got the tip and passed the ball to Howie, who feinted and dribbled out around the foul circle and rifled it to Doodle, standing near the base-line about fifteen feet from the basket. In the most dramatic moment of the tournament, Doodle—holding the ball in his huge, wide-spread hand—leaned far and low to the right, extended his long arm, and started that sweeping motion that signaled the start of his wind-mill shot. Coach Story groaned as he hunched over with arms folded across his stomach as if he were suffering from a cramp. With fear in his voice, he moaned "Oh, no, no! Oh, no, no, please, Doodle. . . . No, not now."

But Doodle was not afraid. In his mind's eye he was back in Pilot Oak, making his perfect windmill hook shots with his *imaginary* ball. When Doodle pitched the basketball that night, it arced perfectly, sailed through the air, and sank through the hoop, hit-ting nothing but the net. The horn blew; the stadium went berserk. Cuba had scratched out an amazing 44-42 victory.

Working his way through the crowd to where Doodle was being mobbed by fans, a red-faced Coach Story shouted, "Doodle! Don't you realize we could have lost the game if you had missed from there?" Struggling to stay upright as fans juggled him onto their shoulders, his face glistening with sweat and happiness, his eyes flooded with tears, Doodle smiled and shouted back: "But, Coach, I didn't *aim* to miss!"

CHAPTER 25

STATE CHAMPIONS 1952

"SPORTS SERVE SOCIETY BY PROVIDING VIVID EXAMPLES OF EXCELLENCE."
—GEORGE F. WILL

Memorial Coliseum—1952. With no time for a much-needed rest after two overtimes, the Cubs prepared themselves for the championship game that evening against Louisville Manual, which had just survived a grueling semifinal game of its own to upset Clark County, 54-53. Clark County and Manual were rated first and second, respectively, in the Associated Press poll that year. Clark County had earlier beaten Cuba, 57-48, and Manual had beaten Cuba twice; the first time, 48-41, and then again in the final game of the Louisville Invitational Tournament, 70-58.

Manual was one of the largest schools in the state and had the tallest players in the tournament. Its stars—six-foot-eight Phil "Cookie" Grawemeyer and six-foot-seven Curtis Moffett—looked like professional players. The average height of Manual's other players was six-foot-four; its smallest players were the same size as Doodle, the tallest Cub. Many sports broadcasters were saying that Cuba was about to meet its nemesis in favored Manual. One radio sportscaster flatly stated, "Cuba doesn't have a Chinaman's chance against the Crimson Tide." Manual had reason to be confident it would beat the Cubs a third time in the championship game, set for 8:45 P.M.

At dusk that Saturday, when the Cubs came out of the hotel to get on the bus for their final ride to Memorial Coliseum, they were shocked to see the Manual team already seated on the bus. The usual procedure was for competing teams to ride in separate buses, but not on this night for some unknown reason.

As the Cubs lined up to board the bus, some Manual fans spotted them and ran over to where they were. Because of all the publicity the media had spread about one man in Cuba staying home to milk all the cows while everyone else went to Lexington, the Manual fans started ringing cowbells and spewing insults about "hicks." Some shouted, "Hey, Cuba, wipe the cow manure off your shoes before you get on the court!" Others yelled, "Yeah, go on home and feed your hogs! Did you have corn pone and taters for supper?" Some were talking loudly about what Manual was going to do with "the skinny little hicks" and they bragged, "The Crimsons are going to mop up the floor tonight with you little hot-doggy hicks. You showoffs!" As the Cubs boarded the bus, none of them responded to the rude remarks. The Manual players didn't say anything either. Everyone just sat quietly looking out the windows.

This trip to Lexington had made the Cubs more sensitive about their humble background. The city had a way of driving the idea of inferiority home to them fast. Dealing with some of the city kids' swaggering sense of superiority and their insults was more than the Cubs needed to handle at that moment. They were tired and tense, and they were facing something bigger than a game. For five years they had been close friends and teammates, living and playing together, dreaming together of winning the state championship. Now all that was ending. Not far ahead lay graduation and the separate paths they would take into adulthood. That game that night was their last game together, and it would mark the end of their boyhood together.

As the bus drove through the narrow streets to the coliseum, the Cubs were silent and tense. The passing street lights and flickering neon signs illuminated the serious expressions on their handsome young faces. Doodle explained:

191

We were country kids in the city. And no matter how many games we won, we were "country." Back in those days there was a distinct difference between city people and country people. When the fact that we were country was pointed out to us, it hurt but it also made us all the more determined to beat them. To show you how green I was, after the Hindman sudden-death, a little kid ran up to me waving a program and asking for my autograph. Hell, I didn't know what he was talking about. Coach Story realized I didn't know and poked me in the ribs with his elbow and said: "Sign your name, boy, that's what the kid wants." So we were green in lots of ways. That night we were to face Manual we were all about as tired and as sad as we have ever been in our lives. After all, this was IT! After we played this game, there'd be no more. We'd be through playing together. We'd graduate and go our separate ways. We had been together since the eighth grade. This championship had been our single goal for five years. Our life together as we had known it was about to end. So, yes, we were sad for many reasons.

That night their sense of humor pulled them through "a lot of heavy stuff" just as it had done many times before. On this final bus ride as the Cubs sat silently, it was Robert Peters, one of their team's managers, who lifted their spirits. Never wanting to be an athlete, Peters always wanted to be a preacher, and he never missed an opportunity to preach. A few months prior to this night, one of his neighbors had given the boy her late husband's Sunday suit, shirt, and tie. Her husband had been a preacher, and Peters said he felt inspired to preach whenever he wore the man's suit. In fact, Peters had taken to dressing up in it and standing outside the Cuba school preaching several mornings a month as the kids came to school.

That night Peters was so upset with the Manual fans' ugly talk that he jumped out of his seat and ran to the front of the bus. Consumed with evangelical zeal, or maybe just pretending he was, he whipped out a frayed Bible from his back pocket and began shouting to the Manual players, *"Repent! Repent! Repent your wicked ways! Your day has come! This is the end for you! Repent!"* His eyes bulged, and his Adam's apple bobbed like a yo-yo as he brandished the Bible and quoted Scripture. Glaring at the Manual players, he shouted, *"This is the final night of your life! Repent! You are wicked! Your time has come, I tell you!"*

The boy's preaching stunned the Manual team and dissolved the Cubs' tension. The Manual players did not laugh, but the Cubs did. Their time had come, also, and they were going to go into it as relaxed as possible. The Manual players just didn't know what to think.

At the coliseum, when it came time for Cuba and Manual to face each other, the organist played "Sweet Georgia Brown" with an enthusiasm that suggested she, also, wanted to see Cuba win. The Cubs ran out onto the floor to a thunder of applause. Only one small section of the stadium was blanketed in red, signifying Manual supporters, and the rest of the entire place was a sea of waving green and gold balloons, pennants, flags, posters, crepe-paper streamers, caps, scarves. The sellout crowd was stamping its feet and screaming, *"Let's Go, Cuba! Let's Go!"* The newspapers reported the next day, "Never in the history of this thirty-five-year-old classic was there a more popular team in Kentucky than Coach Jack Story's Cubs."

As the Cubs looked up and around the arena, they knew that this time they would fulfill their dream. Yet as the game began, it looked like last year's disappointment all over again. Immediately, Manual's Phil Grawemeyer and Curtis Moffett moved their team out to leads of 6-1 and 9-3 in the first four minutes. Howie made a jump shot and Jimmie Webb, a free throw to trim the Manual edge to 13-9, but then Moffett made his free throw and "Duffy" Franklin's long set shot put Manual ahead, 16-9, at the end of the first quarter. Cuba had been able to hit only three of eighteen shots. At the beginning of the second quarter, Doodle made a foul shot. Moffett tipped in a basket and Malcolm Roessler hit a driving shot, doubling

Manual's lead to 20-10. The Cubs fought back but still trailed at halftime, 30-24.

During the halftime break in the locker room, the Cubs circled penitently around Coach Story, looking at him anxiously for help. Without changing the pitch of his voice, he told them: "This is the last time you all will ever play basketball together. After five years of playing together, this is the last time." He shocked them by saying, "So, tonight, you just do what you will please." Without saying another word, he walked away. He had done his coaching and had nothing more to say to them. Doodle angrily said to the others, "I be—damned if we're gonna let Manual beat us!"

As intense as the Cubs were on the court, at least most of the time, the student support off the court sometimes went even a notch higher. This is student-manager Bobby McClain. (Cuba school yearbook photo)

When the Cubs came out for the second-half warm-ups to the snappy beat of their theme song, the arena crowd erupted in a phenomenal display of support. It was as if the crowd sensed what Cuba's last-ditch effort would be like. Lewis Snowden, a member of the Clark County team that had beaten the Cubs for the championship the year before, witnessed it. Snowden said: "I never saw anything like that game before or since. When Cuba came out onto the floor at the half, everybody except the Manual fans stood up and yelled for them. I remember looking around the coliseum, and I saw across the court only one little patch of red sitting in the section for the Manual fans. Everybody else in the whole place was screaming for Cuba to win."

Howie, Doodle, Jimmie, Joe Buddy, and Bill Pollock, who had replaced Raymon, bounded out in the second half with a spirit that only a five-year-old dream could inspire. Like a giant rudely awakened to being robbed, they started their come-from-behind drive that fans were expecting. Bill Pollock started the scoring on a pass from Howie. Grawemeyer followed by hitting one of two foul shots. Joe Buddy made a basket on a pass from Doodle. Then Doodle stole the ball from Moffett and scored. Cuba was now behind only 31-30. The teams exchanged baskets and foul shots on a fairly even basis with Manual staying in front until Joe Buddy scored on a pass from Howie, putting the Cubs ahead for the first time, 41-40. Although Grawemeyer scored one basket before the third quarter ended, Howie and Doodle each contributed a basket and Joe Buddy a free throw to end the quarter with Cuba ahead, 46-42.

The last quarter started with a tip-in by Grawemeyer for Manual. Doodle then rebounded his own shot and Bill Pollock made a basket the same way. Grawemeyer then hit a shot over Doodle's head making the score 50-46. At that point Cuba went into a stall, which many thought was worth the price of admission. For three of the last six minutes, Cuba kept the ball, declining to score and giving up free throws after being fouled by desperate Manual players. With 2:45 left, Jimmie Webb

Doodle is joined by Mary Belle Shelby, one of Cuba's thousands of devotees, outside the Phoenix Hotel in Lexington on the morning after the Cubs' triumph. (Photo courtesy of Charles Floyd)

dashed to the hoop and made a basket. Now it was 52-46, Cuba. Still, there was a long way to go, with plenty of time for the Crimsons to come back, which they started to do when little Neal Skeeters connected from the circle, cutting Cuba's lead to 52-48. Moffett followed with a tip-in before Doodle answered for Cuba with a lay-in at the 1:38 mark. A little over thirty seconds later, Moffett streaked in for an easy hoop, cutting Cuba's lead to 54-52 with only 1:03 left.

In a grandstand performance, Doodle made another bucket with 52 seconds left, putting Cuba back up by four, 56-52, with Manual unable to score on its next possession. There were only forty seconds left to play. For those last forty seconds, the crowd,

The late-winter chill of a convertible ride through Kentucky is a small inconvenience for Coach Story and Howie Crittenden as they show off the 1952 state championship trophy. (Photo courtesy of Howie Crittenden)

except for Manual fans, was screaming as loud as it could in unison with the Cuba cheerleaders, "*Hey! Hey! What'da you say! Cuba! Cuba! All the way!*" Cuba went back into its stall and gave the ball to, who else, Howie.

The waning moments were sweet. While Manual went after Howie with increasing desperation, he retreated down long paths of trial and experience. He led Manual across worn patches of country clay and creaky country gym floors. He led it down miles of dusty country roads and through all those winter days and summer nights of practice at home in Graves County. He led them farther than Manual could follow. In the last eighteen seconds, Jimmie Webb sneaked in for a basket, making the final score Cuba 58, Manual 52.

Cuba's dream season was now complete, and somewhere on press row Larry Shropshire must have burned.

EPILOGUE

At the closing ceremony of the 1952 state tournament, Howie and Doodle, for the second straight year, were among the ten boys chosen for the All-State Tournament Team. Linville Puckett from Clark County was selected for the third straight year. The other Kentucky greats were Phil Grawemeyer from Manual and his teammates Curtis Moffett and Neal Skeeters. Also named were Garnard Martin from Hindman, Jerry Bird from Corbin, Robert Anderson from Henry Clay, and Carlos Irwin of Breckenridge County.

The Cubs' trip home was a triumphant procession. As they moved through the state, word of their arrival spread before them. People in the towns and tiny communities along the route packed the streets to wave flags and to cheer them. At Horse Cave in central Kentucky, a local hotel owner treated them to steak dinners. In Trigg County, 750 fans met them with convertibles, and at Eggner's Ferry Bridge this time the welcoming crowd was estimated at 4,000. The motorcade from the bridge to Mayfield stretched for fourteen miles. In the courthouse square an estimated 12,000 stood patiently in the cold weather to greet the team. When the convoy finally squeezed into the square, the cheering lasted more than fifteen minutes.

Again, there was a microphone and another round of speech making. Coach Story was not as emotional as he had been during the posttournament ceremony the previous year; he simply said, "I'm mighty glad we could bring back the trophy." Then each player said a few words. When his turn came, Howie couldn't hold back his tears. In a trembling voice, he said, "There are two things I am proud of today. First, we won the tournament, and second, Mr. Story said we made him feel like a young mule."

The following week the Cubs toured the Jackson Purchase, showing off their championship trophy. The purpose behind the tour was to inspire other high school teams to set goals and to work hard at achieving them. The slogan in the region was "Let's build our teams next season so that we can keep the trophy west of the Tennessee River!"

The forty-car motorcade, led by state troopers, covered all of the Jackson Purchase, starting with Sedalia, then on to Mayfield, Farmington, Murray, Almo, Hardin, Benton, Sharpe, Reidman, Paducah, Kevil, La Center, Barlow, Wickliffe, Bardwell, Arlington, Clinton, Fulgham, Fulton, Dukedom, Pilot Oak, and ending in Cuba. Doodle was the only Cub not present for the tour. Sadly, he was home ill, suffering from a cold, fever, and exhaustion.

On the following Monday night, an Open House-Appreciation Supper at the Cuba school was held in honor of the champions. The little building was crammed with more than two thousand people, some of whom had driven many miles to attend the celebration. Every inch of space in the gym, in the front hall, and in the class-rooms that opened onto the gym was jam-packed. Ted Bradley's dad, Marshall, was the master of ceremonies that night, and he introduced Coach Story first.

As the coach introduced the team, he handed each boy a handsome reversible green and gold jacket that had the state championship emblem on the back and another emblem on the sleeve, indicating the Cubs had been the runners-up in the 1951 state tournament. He then presented to Dr. J. T. Fuller, the team's physician, a plaque in appreciation of his services. After making a brief talk, Dr. Fuller gave Coach Story and each player a certificate for a suit of clothes, donated by Reece's Style Mart and the Curlee Clothing Company. With money he collected from Mayfield merchants and individuals, Wayne Morgan of WKTM radio station in Mayfield gave each player a wristwatch and a necktie.

The main speaker that night was Flavious B. Martin, the commonwealth attorney since 1922. Born and reared in Cuba, Martin praised the little community for its outstanding support for its

team, and he extolled the Cubs' magnificent display of sportsmanship and determination to win.

Then Marshall Bradley, the master of ceremonies, introduced
the coaches in the audience. College coaches in attendance included Harlan Hodges of Murray State, Ed Diddle of Western
Kentucky, and Gene Lambert of Memphis State. Noticeably absent
were representatives from the University of Kentucky and the University of Louisville. In their brief remarks all of the coaches said
how much they would like to have the Cubs on their college teams
the next fall.

Coach Diddle invited Howie and Doodle to be members of
his Kentucky All-Star team that was to play the Indiana All-Stars
the next summer at Indianapolis. He also urged the two boys to
enroll at Western and play on his squad.

Dr. Ralph Woods, the president of Murray State Teachers College, congratulated the team and the community and evoked laughter when he added how nice it would be to see some of the Cuba
Cubs' faces at Murray State in the fall. He made it plain, too, that
the Cuba stars would be invited to play with the South All-Stars in
Murray's annual North-South cage classic in June.

After all the speech making was done that night, everyone was
treated to a barbecue supper, complete with all the trimmings, including homemade breads and desserts. The supper was prepared
by the Cuba homemakers and farmers and volunteers from Mayfield. It was Cuba's way of saying "Thanks to everyone!"

*   *   *

Coach Diddle came to Pilot Oak to visit with Howie and Doodle
in their homes and to talk to them and to their parents, but he
failed to convince either boy to come to Western Kentucky to play
for his team. Both boys had many offers from other colleges but no
guidance in how to choose among the offers. Coach Story never
advised or even talked to them about selecting a college. When
some politicians offered Howie a full scholarship to Murray State,
along with many other perks, including a promise to give his dad a

job with the highway department, Howie accepted. Doodle was also given a full scholarship to Murray State, plus the perks. Going along with them were Joe Buddy, Jimmie Webb, Don Poyner, and Bobby McClain. Except for Doodle, all of them graduated with bachelor's and master's degrees in education and went on to have successful careers in education—as coaches, physical education or social studies teachers, principals, and administrators.

After a year at Murray, Doodle transferred to Northeast Mississippi Junior College in Booneville, Mississippi, where, in 1954, he led the nation in scoring with an average of thirty-eight points a game. From there, he went to Mississippi Southern (now called Southern Mississippi) and played basketball for a year until he suffered a serious back injury. After having back surgery he was so disabled, he had to withdraw from school. While still recuperating, he applied for an emergency teaching certificate (such certificates were given in those days under certain circumstances). He taught history and physical education at Farmington High School in Graves County for a year. Then he moved again to accept an offer to play for Mississippi College in Clinton, Mississippi. But his nagging back problems caused him to withdraw after a year. He went to work for Reynolds Aluminum in Phoenix, Arizona, playing on the Reynolds basketball team in an American Amateur Union basketball league. There, again, his back problems prevented him from playing basketball the way he once had. At that point, he gave up trying to play. He moved to Knoxville, Tennessee, where he married Mary Lou Martin and opened an industrialized painting company. Until he retired in 1998, he operated this successful business. He and Mary still live in Knoxville. Their two sons, both grown, live in Knoxville, too. One is in the construction business, the other is a golf pro. Several times a year, Doodle visits his brother Bill, who still lives in their old homeplace in Pilot Oak. He loves rambling around the countryside in Graves County and talking with the old-timers.

After teaching in several high schools in western Kentucky, Howie became principal of Calloway County High School in

Murray, Kentucky. He was there from 1966 to 1974. Then he moved to Henderson, Kentucky, where he became the principal of Henderson County Senior High School. After he retired from that position in 1995, he took a temporary job in a large law firm that was opening offices in various cities in Kentucky. He supervised staff and functioned as a coordinator for these offices until they became established. Now he occasionally works as a substitute principal in the Bowling Green area. Twice divorced, he now lives with Meg, his third wife, in Bowling Green. He has one son, Howie Jr., from his first marriage. On March 14, 1989, Howard was inducted into the Kentucky High School Athletic Association Hall of Fame. Others also inducted that night were golfer Gay Brewer, a former Masters champion; former NBA great Wes Unseld, currently head coach of the Washington Bullets; former NFL official Tommy Bell; and ex-Boston Celtic star Frank Ramsey. With the same rare blend of confidence and modesty he had as a child, Crittenden said that night, "Just to be mentioned along with those people is quite an honor." And he added that he had invited his Cuba Cubs teammates to share the event with him because, "Without them, I wouldn't be receiving this honor."

*   *   *

Jimmie Webb and Martha Layne Casey, who married in September 1951, in their senior year of high school, expect to celebrate their fiftieth wedding anniversary. They are as much in love with each other today as they were in high school. They have two grown children and three grandchildren. Their daughter Terri Webb Wolf is an elementary school teacher in Louisville, and their son Jeff, who was football coach at the University of Illinois, is now football coach at the University of Northern Alabama. Jimmie and Martha live in Teutopolis, Illinois, where Jimmie was for many years the principal of a junior high school.

*   *   *

Shortly after Donald Poyner received his master's degree from Murray State and while he was working as an administrator in the

202

Graves County school system, he organized and managed a men's semipro softball team that competed in the American Softball Association. His team played 110 games a year for a five-year period, and it holds the national record for winning five straight regional championships. Donald and his wife, Dortha, live in Mayfield, where he is the assistant superintendent of Graves County Schools. They have two daughters.

*   *   *

After high school graduation, Bill Pollock joined the navy. After a stint in the service, he worked in Michigan for a while. Then he moved back to Mayfield, married, and went to work in the sheriff's office. He was chief deputy for four years before he quit to work for the municipal gas department. In 1981 he opened his own plumbing business, which he still owns and operates. He and his wife have three children and four grandchildren.

Mason Harris, a team manager, lives in Cottage Grove, Tennessee, where he works for a pipeline company as a mechanic. He and his wife, Betty Jane, have two sons.

Jimmy Brown and Joe Buddy Warren, both retired, live in Mayfield. Jimmy was for many years a salesman for a tobacco company. Joe Buddy, who was an assistant girls' basketball coach at Graves County High School, spends most of his time now on the golf course.

A retired school administrator, Bobby McClain and his family live on his big farm outside of Cuba, where he is very active in his church.

After serving in the military during the Korean war, Ted Bradley became a tractor-trailer truck driver for years. He's retired and lives near Murray. He and Joe Buddy occasionally hunt and fish together just as they did as boys.

*   *   *

Raymon McClure married while he was a junior in high school, and he and his wife lived on a farm near Sedalia. Raymon died in

203

his late forties in a tragic silo accident. Robert Peters and Paul Boyd Simpson are gone, too. Robert died in his early thirties of a brain tumor and Paul in an automobile accident in the early 1980s. At the time of his death, Paul had just retired from naval service and had returned to live in Graves County. Harold Roberts farmed in the Cuba area and worked as a bricklayer and carpenter. He died in his late fifties of cancer.

*   *   *

Helen Crittenden, Howie's twin sister, a Cuba cheerleader, married Jones Glover when she was a junior in high school. They had one child, a son, and lived in Mayfield, where Helen worked as a medical secretary for several physicians. Helen died in an automobile accident just outside of Mayfield one summer afternoon in 1996.

Coach Story received many honors for leading the Cuba Cubs to victory. He was named head coach for the West in the first annual East-West game, which was played as part of the University of Kentucky athletic clinic in August 1952, and he was also selected to head a group of high school all-stars in games across the state. After the Cubs graduated from high school and left for college, Story also left Cuba to become head basketball coach at Mayfield High School. He took Mayfield to the state tournament three times—in 1955, 1956, and 1962—but never again brought home the championship. Many of Story's players went on to play college basketball. His own son Rex, an outstanding athlete, played on the 1955–56 team and made All-State.

Story became known as the "dean" of western Kentucky basketball. He won 478 games in his coaching career and never had a losing season. In the early 1960s, after he began having serious problems with his balance and speech, he was told that he had an inoperable brain tumor. When he had to retire from coaching in the fall of 1965, he philosophized, "I guess I have realized about everything a coach could want in basketball."

Jack Story faced his greatest challenge with the same courage and quietness that he taught his basketball players to have. He died at ten o'clock on the morning of September 8, 1971, at Baptist Memorial Hospital in Memphis, Tennessee. He was only fifty-four years old. With him were the ones he loved best, his wife, Mary Lee, his daughters Carolyn and Barbara, and son Rex. He was buried in Highland Park Cemetery in Mayfield. One of the pallbearers at his funeral was Howie Crittenden. His wife, who never remarried, died in August 1998.

*　　*　　*

The little Cuba schoolhouse where the Cubs' dream was born has long since been torn down. In 1977 it was replaced with "a modern, progressive facility, with certified faculty and administrators, and with a much-improved curriculum and athletic facilities." Since then, nothing remarkable has happened in Cuba. The little community no longer looks the way it did when the Cubs were attending school there. It is neither lively nor thriving. The large oak trees that once lined the main road and shaded the homes are all gone. In their places are a few old trailers, automobiles, and trucks in various stages of disrepair. On what were once some well-kept lawns are now parts of farm machinery, lawn mowers, piles of lumber, and other stuff. Where blackberries, lilacs, and rose bushes grew in abundance can now occasionally be found discarded soft-drink cans, fast-food cartons, and empty plastic milk containers—symbols of our culture now.

Nearly all of the original houses and barns are gone, and the dirt roads that the boys ran up and down, tossing and dribbling basketballs, are overgrown with weeds. Many of the people who live in the Cuba area now don't know everyone else there by first name. In the evenings they don't sit on their front porches and talk as the folks once did. Missing, too, from the landscape, are little boys playing basketball outside.

Rhodes's, one of the two general stores where the village folk used to congregate and have so much fun, where the store setters teased and the checkers games went on every day, where the folks gathered to listen to the ball games on Fred Rhodes's radio, is now an abandoned, run-down building. The other store, Harper's, where the teenagers used to gather, where the boys played basketball every afternoon, no longer exists.

Dr. Page's little office is still standing—silent, dusty, with dry leaves scattered about on the floor. His black leather examining table is there, too, and the waiting room's straight-back wooden chairs still line the walls. His large black record books, with patients' names and receipts written in his strong clear handwriting, are strewn about on the table in the back room he used as his office and pharmacy. Some of the little white envelopes he used to blow into, to open, lie on the shelf.

Off in the grassy fields, a few cisterns and neglected old smokehouses with rusty netless basketball goals nailed to the sides are silent reminders of days long gone.

In the last fifty years, small schools have been consolidated into larger ones, despite objections from parents, students, and teachers. With their schools gone, many little rural communities—like Cuba—have lost their sense of identity, unity, and purpose. They are as fragmented now as cities are, so it is not likely that little Cuba's story will ever happen again. And that magical kind of euphoria that Cuba created—a euphoria that did not quickly vanish after the tournament as sports' highs do today—also has, perhaps, disappeared from the American scene.

Cuba, its spirited little team and coach, showed us what imagination, determination, and hard work can do. Cuba's story is the American dream.

The Cuba Cubs
1951–52 Kentucky State
High School Basketball Champions

First row, seated on floor: managers Robert Peters, Rex Story, and Bobby McClain. Second row: Paul Simpson, Jimmy Brown, Joe Buddy Warren, Howie Crittenden, Jimmy Sims, and Ted Bradley. Third row: Coach Jack Story, Raymon McClure, Bill Pollock, Doodle Floyd, Harold Roberts, Drennon Bagwell, Jimmie Webb, and assistant coach Joe McPherson. (Cuba school yearbook photo)

Alma Mater

In the heart of the Jackson Purchase
'neath the sun's warm glow
Lies the home of dear old Cuba,
sweetest name I know.
May we cherish our traditions,
wave the banner high.
May our love for dear old Cuba
live and never die.

BIBLIOGRAPHY

Kindred, Dave. *Basketball: The Dream Game in Kentucky.* (Data Courier, Inc.: Louisville), 1976.

Kleber, John E. Ed. *The Kentucky Encyclopedia.* (University of Kentucky: Lexington, Kentucky), 1992.

Miller, Don. *The Carr Creek Legacy.* (Vantage Press: New York), 1995.

Rice, Russell. *The Wildcat Legacy.* (JCP Corp: Virginia Beach, Virginia), 1982.